COPS 'N' ROBBERS

COPS 'N' ROBBERS

HILARIOUS TRUE STORIES OF BUNGLING BURGLARS AND CRAFTY COPPERS

BY **Matthew Ventham**
AND **Stephen Brennan**

JOHN BLAKE

Published by John Blake Publishing Limited Ltd,
3, Bramber Court, 2 Bramber Road,
London W14 9PB, England

www.blake.co.uk

First published in paperback in 2003

ISBN 1 84454 008 1

British Library Cataloguing-in-Publication Data:

A catalogue record for this book is available
from the British Library.

Design by www.envydesign.co.uk

Printed in Great Britain by BookMarque

1 3 5 7 9 10 8 6 4 2

Papers used by John Blake Publishing are natural, recyclable
products made from wood grown in sustainable forests.
The manufacturing processes conform to the environmental
regulations of the country of origin.

Any opinions expressed within this book are those of the authors
and not those of the British police service.

Matt dedicates this book to his wife, Sarah-Jane Ventham-Pouffier and to the loving memory of Arthur Ventham.

Steve dedicates this book to his brother, Danny, and to Sarah Jane Harvey.

CONTENTS

INTRODUCTION

COPS 'N' ROBBERS was inspired by a rather unpleasant off-duty incident that happened to the pair of us, causing us both to question whether or not the police was indeed our suited career. After some discussion and several bottles of red wine, we decided to stick with it, since giving villains a hard time – coupled with a daily dose of the police's unique humour – still succeeded in making it all worthwhile. After several weeks of whingeing we decided to channel our energies into something more positive and made a drunken pledge to gather as many true tales from within the inner sanctum as we possibly could and present them for the enjoyment of members of the public and police alike.

The following collection of funny police tales has therefore been collected, written and edited by ourselves. They consist of stories that derive from our own experiences and those of other British police officers, both serving and retired. The current climate of political correctness has made it very difficult to construct this book. Despite this, however, all the contributors have retained a healthy sense of humour and we find it encouraging that such humour still prevails within the rank and file of the modern British police service. If you enjoy reading *Cops 'n' Robbers* half as much as we have enjoyed putting it together, then we have achieved our objective.

This book would not have been possible but for the generosity, good will and support of all our fellow officers, who took the time and effort to send us material and letters of encouragement. You have our thanks. We would like to dedicate this book to all officers, both retired and serving, who believe that a criminal's home is Her Majesty's Prison and who genuinely joined to make a difference. We would like to encourage anyone who is thinking of joining the police to do so, as it is

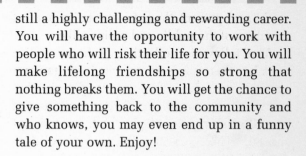

still a highly challenging and rewarding career. You will have the opportunity to work with people who will risk their life for you. You will make lifelong friendships so strong that nothing breaks them. You will get the chance to give something back to the community and who knows, you may even end up in a funny tale of your own. Enjoy!

Matthew Ventham
Stephen Brennan
August 2003

CHAPTER ONE

COPPERS AND VILLAINS

The relationship between copper and criminal is a strange one that can vary from mutual respect to outright hatred. The following chapter however, just goes to show how similar these two strange strains of humanity can be when it comes to stupidity and balls-ups. Some of the names have been changed to protect the idiotic.

In 1947 PC Cooper, formerly a D-Day commando, had only just been posted to Southgate in Middlesex when he and a colleague were sent to deal with a man reported to be climbing in through a house window. Rushing to the scene, the two PCs indeed found a window wide open and they quickly entered the premises in the hope that the intruder was still inside. Sure enough, hearing a noise they raced upstairs, where they found a young man taking clothes from the wardrobe. Without much ado they weighed in and the man was dragged downstairs struggling and protesting. Congratulating themselves on the rare feat of having caught a burglar in the act, it was only back at the station that it was established that their prisoner was in fact the son of the house, home unexpectedly on leave, who had lost his key, let himself in through the window and was busy unpacking his suitcase when two burly coppers jumped him. The man later commented good humouredly, 'I haven't had such a good fight in ages.'

A Thames Valley PC was part of a large strength of officers drafted in to deal with the Greenham Common anti-nuclear missile demonstrations of the 1980s. Police faced a torrent of abuse from militant females, most of whom had been living in tents for weeks and smelt like it. He and his colleagues received orders to link arms and were told that on no account were they to break the chain – to do so would involve being disciplined. At this point a smelly female demonstrator decided to put her hand down her knickers and pull out her tampon, which she then threw at the helpless PC. Glancing down, he saw glistening on his shoulder an object with its string trailing onto his shirt. He was then heard to say, 'Please God, let that be a tea bag.'

An unlucky thief out on his midnight prowl had a surprise when he decided to lever open the back doors of a home computer delivery van. As the doors sprang open, he was confronted by three burly PCs in full uniform drinking coffee. Of the ten vans in the car park he had chosen the police surveillance van. Dropping the crowbar in shock, he said, 'I'm nicked, aren't I?' To which the three smiling coppers replied, 'Yes, we think you are.' As he was dragged into the van, he mumbled, 'You weren't the sort of PCs I was after.'

A drunken yob seriously assaulted a male in a Hammersmith nightclub and ran from police, making his getaway across the rooftops of some nearby shops. He was

3

laughing as he escaped across the various rooftops, blue lights flashing in the distance. He then came to a large gap and decided that, even with his alcohol-induced confidence, he wouldn't be able to jump the gap. He therefore decided to try and find a way down. The yob managed to open a roof door, and began lowering himself through a skylight. As he lowered his body through, he slipped and fell ten feet onto a large wooden desk, which crumpled on impact. Unhurt and rather pleased with himself, he sat up and glanced to his right. There stood the custody sergeant of Hammersmith Police Station with a broad grin on his face. 'Nice of you to drop in,' sneered the sergeant. Unfortunately, the yob had chosen the skylight of Hammersmith Police Station as his escape route.

Police caught a well-known heroin addict climbing out of an old person's bungalow at two in the morning, his emaciated, needle-marked arms clutching a TV. Knowing full well that with his considerable criminal record he would probably go to prison, he said to the officers, 'I don't suppose you would believe me if I told you I was only borrowing it?'

Having punched his girlfriend in the face, a dim teenage villain decided to escape on a child's BMX pedal bike. PC Brennan, who was on the scene, sprinted after the youth, who was pedalling as fast as he could. Due to a combination of lack of fitness, and the scorching summer sun beating down, he quickly ran out of energy, allowing PC Brennan to gain ground. Despite repeated shouts for him to stop, he pedalled on. Other officers joined the chase as the suspect cycled furiously down the road. Catching up, PC Brennan managed to pull him off the bike, causing PC, suspect and bike to crash to the floor in a painful heap. 'Why didn't you stop?' PC Brennan demanded as he lifted the sweating, winded youth up from the concrete. Desperate for an excuse for trying to escape, the teenager replied, 'I didn't have any lights on my bike.'

One Christmas Eve a thief who had just been charged with stealing a charity box said to the custody sergeant, 'Well, there's gotta be some give and take at Christmas, ain't there?'

Police surrounded a boat on the River Thames in Surrey following a report of a mentally ill male armed with a handgun. PC Mike Middleton and PC Rob Bowden positioned themselves behind a wall and were told to observe the boat in case the male tried to leave the area prior to the arrival of the armed police unit. PC Middleton peered over the wall and saw the suspect climbing up on to the deck of the boat. He quickly shouted down his radio, 'Priority, priority! All units, the suspect is armed with a crossbow. Repeat, suspect is armed with a crossbow!' A deathly silence followed over the air as various officers frantically tried to find cover. Seconds later the radio silence was broken by a rather sheepish PC Middleton: 'Cancel my last ... it's a music stand.' PC Middleton was last seen diving for cover at the London Symphony Orchestra.

A stressed female radio controller was requesting various police units to attend a large pub fight. All the police units responded at once. 'Charlie 1, we are in the area we will head towards.' 'Roger that, Charlie 1,' she replied. 'Charlie 2, we'll back up on the last.' 'Roger that, Charlie 2.' Another unit then called up: 'Charlie X-ray ...' The stressed controller,

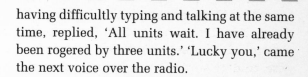

having difficultly typing and talking at the same time, replied, 'All units wait. I have already been rogered by three units.' 'Lucky you,' came the next voice over the radio.

A suspect for an assault attended a police station in Devon having returned on bail to stand on an identification parade. The evidence against him was very thin - in fact it was anorexic, and he knew it. He had denied the offence and knew all the legal loopholes. With his solicitor present, the suspect spent some time selecting his position in the line-up. Eventually he made his choice standing between two people that looked the most like him. The video camera was started and the witness to the assault was directed into the room. On entering the room the elderly witness paused to put on her glasses, whereupon the suspect shouted, 'She wasn't wearing glasses the other day.' His solicitor advised him to change his story and plead guilty.

Greater Manchester PC, Ann Davies, who was known to have worked in IT during her previous employment, was asked by CID to try and find out who owned a computer that they had seized during a morning police raid on a villain's address. Keen to impress the plain-clothes officers, PC Davies spent hours trying to access files on the computer, to no avail. She didn't have a clue what she was doing, as all she had ever done was input information, but she wasn't about to admit to it. The shift ended and another officer took over the onerous task. The following day, PC Davies was curious to see if the computer had been identified. A CID officer informed her that they had located the owner, which was a local school. Intrigued, PC Davies asked how they found out, to which the CID officer replied, 'Easy, we looked under-neath and read the label.'

A young villain who had recently come out of prison told Humberside PC Michael Hugill that drugs were just as easily come by in prison as out of prison. PC Hugill asked him if the drugs cost more in prison. He replied, 'No, the price was just the same as outside, but you only got half as much.' PC Hugill later suggested to the lad's probation officer that he avoid any job in the field of sales.

Safety-conscious Special Constable Jill Law was called to a large fight in Stanstead. On arrival she found several drunken males fighting, one of whom was holding a lit cigarette as he pushed and swore at another male. Approaching the aggressive male, she said to him, 'Give me that. You might hurt someone.' The male handed her the cigarette saying, 'Oh right, thanks,' before proceeding to punch the male in front of him unconscious.

During a busy shift in a London police station, two senior officers carrying out a security survey entered the control room and stood behind the staff discussing upgrading the CCTV monitors that displayed pictures of the rear gates to the station. One of the officers, a pedantic chief inspector, interrupted one of the PCs and asked if there were any problems with the CCTV. The PC informed the two officers that the picture was fine. Okay, said the chief inspector, 'So who is that coming into the rear yard?' The PC, looking at the screen, correctly identified a female member of the staff. 'Ah,' said the man, 'you obviously know her. If the next person to come through the gates is a complete stranger, who you have never seen before, with these outdated monitors, would you be able to recognise her?' 'No,' agreed the PC, 'but if this complete stranger came into the yard up the stairs and into this control room, I still wouldn't bloody recognise them, would I?' With that the chief inspector from Security and his bagman exited stage left.

A police control room operator received an incident message on his screen from the traffic control stating that there had been a personal injury road traffic accident and that a Doctor who was passing had stopped to help. Further down the incident log some wag had added that the Cybermen were assisting with vehicle recovery.

One particular night around 3 a.m., the alarm was activated at a newsagent in Basildon, Essex, and police duly attended at best speed. On arrival PC Mark Shaw could see the alarm box flashing but the alarm itself was silent. As the front of the premises was secure he went around to the back, where he found a local villain, Richard, leaning against the wall of the shop. Although he seemed to be looking directly at him as the officer approached, Richard almost jumped out of his skin when PC Shaw said 'Hello.' A voice calling from inside the enclosed yard of the shop was then heard, so Richard was handed over to a colleague and, in heroic style, PC Shaw leapt over the wall. There he found Richard's partner in crime, David, clutching several boxes of cigarettes while trying in vain to scale the eight-foot wall. Both males were arrested and taken to the police station.

In interview, it transpired that they had been working for another well-known thief who had enlisted the services of Richard and David because he was on a curfew from court and couldn't risk going out, as he was too recognisable. This sounded like a good plan until you realise that Richard, who had been tasked with the job of lookout, was totally blind in one eye, partially sighted in the other and wore glasses that must have been cut from the bottoms of two milk bottles. As for David, well, David had been given the job of the runner; however, David was in fact pretty much crippled since a road accident and struggled to get up a kerb, let alone an eight-foot wall.

A PC on night duty in Staffordshire responded to a mundane call concerning a set of temporary traffic lights that a passing motorist had reported as being permanently stuck on red. On attending he found that this was indeed the case but due to the time of night was unable to contact the local authority. As a short-term solution, and to avoid early morning traffic congestion, the PC decided to turn the traffic lights around, realising that they were not needed at this hour anyway. Forgetting to inform anyone of his temporary measure, he returned from leave some days later and was informed that some vandal had interfered with the traffic lights, causing all the trains on the nearby tracks to stop and resulting in commuter chaos.

PC Lucas and his colleague were called to a report of a violent shoplifter in a Sutton store who had been detained. On arrival the thief, who was a large shaven-headed yob, decided to fight and after a brief struggle was put to the floor and handcuffed. He was taken to custody complaining that officers had broken his ankle and demanded to be taken to hospital. All present knew this wasn't the case, but the custody sergeant, not willing to risk his pension, instructed the PCs to convey the injured male to hospital just in case.

The yob, who was well known for play-acting, continued to rub his foot and made a great show of telling everyone in the hospital foyer what police had done to him, while he sat his wheelchair. After a lengthy wait a doctor examined him and predictably declared that he could find nothing wrong. The disgruntled officers then wheeled the patient out of the examination room, where the smiling yob gave them a smug wink and said, 'Wasted a couple of your f*cking hours, didn't it?' Before the officers could think of a suitable reply a patient in another wheelchair crashed into the yob's extended leg, fracturing his ankle painfully in three places. What goes around comes around.

Following a burglary in a stately home, the well-to-do house owner decided to lend officers his metal detector, as the thief had discarded a large amount of jewellery across the grounds. An ex-squaddie PC then began to scan the croquet lawn with the metal detector. Surprised at how often the detector beeped he dug numerous holes all over the lawn but was unable to find any jewellery. Seven holes later the distressed house owner pointed out that the PC was wearing steel-toe-capped boots.

A new civilian call handler was inputting a crime onto the police computer for a PC over the phone. Her colleague overheard her asking the officer how to spell the victim's name, 'Regina'. When questioned about this she commented that the family known as Regina must be really unlucky, since this was the third time in a week that they had been a victim of crime. Her colleague then explained to the inexperienced call handler that 'Regina' was used when the victim of crime was, in fact, the Crown. 'Oh I see,' she replied.

An out-of-breath PC was chasing a male who had just robbed someone at knifepoint. As he ran, he desperately tried to give a commentary over the radio and put out a description of the suspect. He described the male as being black, six foot tall and armed with a three-inch lock knife. Due to the PC's shortness of breath and the poor radio reception, he was forced to repeat the description several times. The female radio operator then came on over the air and said, 'All I'm getting is three inches', to which a voice responded, 'Well, stand on a box then.'

The calm of a Christmas night was broken one year in London when three drunks decided it would be a good idea to climb up the Norwegian Christmas tree in Trafalgar Square. The tree was swaying under the combined weight of the three reckless males as Sgt Maloney arrived, accompanied by a PC. Seeing the police arrive, the drunks immediately began shouting tirades of abuse at the officers some thirty feet below and refused to come down. It was at this point that a police dog handler arrived, his Alsatian straining at the leash. The sergeant then shouted, 'If you lads don't come down here now, I'll send the dog up to get you.' At this the drunken males climbed quickly down and were placed into custody. As they were being handcuffed, the dog handler patted his dog and, turning to the sergeant, said, 'So we've trained the f*ckers to climb up trees now, have we?'

PC Alan Ingram, a dog handler, was on football duty at a Bristol City vs Millwall game in 1983. There was crowd trouble both inside and outside the ground and both he and other dog handlers were deployed just outside the City ground to keep the warring factions apart. A group of Millwall supporters then began attacking a smaller group of City fans and PC Ingram went in with his trusty Alsatian, Bruce, to try to break it up. Bruce, not known for his gentle ways, was ready for anything, and after numerous police warnings to stop fighting, he shot forward, clamping his jaws onto the backside of a City hooligan, who screamed, 'That dog's an animal!' Minutes later, in the interests of fairness, Bruce bit a fighting Millwall supporter hard on the thigh. The yob was arrested for affray and replied after caution, 'I'm going to sue that dog!'

Around ten years ago, Chris Down, then a trainee detective constable, was sent with a colleague to search a house for a prolific burglar. Attending the address, the occupier tipped off the officers that the suspect was indeed hiding upstairs somewhere in the premises. Running up the stairs, DC Down and his colleague proceeded to search the whole house. They looked under the beds, behind cabinets and in the airing cupboard before coming to a large wooden wardrobe in the last bedroom to be searched. DC Down yanked the door open to reveal the burglar standing there with his hands over his eyes as if hoping that by doing so he would somehow remain invisible. As the miscreant slowly lifted one hand then the other from his face, DC Down remarked, 'What, you on your way back from Narnia?' to which the burglar, apparently having missed out on the delights of C S Lewis, responded, 'What the f*ck are you talking about?' 'Never mind,' replied the grinning DC, 'You're nicked.'

Many years ago in a London police station a police officer was given a severe beating by a violent criminal, as a result of which he suffered serious injuries. His colleagues spent the rest of the night trying to track down the culprit, who had been named and was well known to them. On locating him, a second fight ensued but due to sufficient police numbers the man was arrested and successfully brought, bruised and battered, before the custody sergeant, who threw him straight into a cell.

Later that evening, the offender was brought out and stood before the custody inspector ready for charging. 'I hear you've given one of mine a right good seeing to tonight,' said the inspector, quietly. 'Yeah,' came the reply, 'you f*cking want some as well?' Without a further word, the inspector picked up his heavy-duty typewriter and flung it at the offender, hitting him square in the chest and knocking him to the ground. The offender was later charged with grievous bodily harm to the officer. He was also charged with criminal damage to the typewriter. Strangely enough, the offender pleaded guilty to both charges.

A Cheshire housewife looked out of her kitchen window one afternoon to see a man taking tools from her neighbour's white transit van. She saw that the window of the van had been smashed. Concerned, she immediately called police on her mobile phone and went out to confront the male. The man told her that he was just helping his friend out. This was relayed to the police operator, who told her police were unable to attend. The operator then said, 'Let me speak to him and we'll sort this matter out.' The lady then passed the phone to the man, who told the operator that his mate's van had recently been damaged and that he was just removing the tools until his friend returned so they wouldn't get nicked. The phone was then handed back to the housewife, who was confidently told by the operator, Don't worry miss. This lad's kosher.'

Two hours later the neighbour returned to find that his van had been broken into and his tools stolen. The police operator is now working at a drive-thru McDonald's.

Two PCs attended a burglary in Northumbria at which a large rock had been used to smash the patio doors and effect entry. The victim had left the rock in situ in the belief that there may be fingerprints. Picking up the rock, and out of the victim's earshot, the PC turned to his colleague and said, 'Idiot. As if we can get fingerprints off that.' He then tossed the thing out through the patio windows into the garden. Unfortunately, the glazier had just replaced the glass.

Sgt Glen Jones was in the Gillingham police canteen when a call came out over the air: 'CID officers require urgent assistance.' Jumping to their feet, Sgt Jones and PC Les

Roberts rushed out and headed towards the destination at breakneck speed. PC Roberts drove as Sgt Jones, operating the two tones (siren and blue light) held on for dear life. The rain was bucketing down and visibility was poor as PC Roberts skidded round blind bends, narrowly missing oncoming traffic and the occasional pedestrian. The windscreen wipers, although on double speed, could hardly cope with the torrent of rain and the Saturday afternoon traffic was horrendous. Seconds away from the location, they were cancelled. Slowing right down they turned round and headed back, pulse rates slowly getting back to normal. PC Roberts then said, 'Sarge, reach into the back seat under my coat, will you?' Sgt Jones replied, 'Yeah. What is it you want?' PC Roberts replied, 'My glasses, I can't see a f*cking thing without them.'

A regular visitor to Staines Police Station was once more brought before the custody sergeant. Looking wearily at the ageing villain the sergeant said, 'You must know every policeman around here.' 'I certainly do, Sarge,' the villain sighed, 'but the trouble is, the older ones have all retired and the younger ones can run faster.'

20

A West Midlands DC called Stan and his colleague went to the house of a local villain who was known both to his associates and to police as Fuzzy Bear, on account of his huge size and fearsome temper. Fuzzy Bear had managed to keep himself out of trouble for some years. In fact, it was not unknown for Fuzzy to physically assist local police whenever younger offenders thought they would have a go. Stan was faced with the daunting task of having to arrest Fuzzy's little brother, Joey, for a recent burglary on an old people's home. Knocking on the door, Stan asked Fuzzy if he could speak to Joey. Fuzzy asked why the officers wanted Joey and Stan thought it prudent to tell him. Fuzzy told them, 'Wait there,' and slammed the door. They then heard Fuzzy bellow from inside, 'Joey, have you been thieving again?' 'No, Fuzz, honest.' 'I've told you to stop thieving Joey.' 'I ain't been thieving Fuzz, honest Fuzz.' The officers then heard the sound of two sets of clumping feet as first Joey, then Fuzzy, ran up the stairs. 'I've told you what would happen if I found out you'd been stealing,' roared Fuzzy. There then followed a dull thump followed by a loud 'Oooof'. Suddenly the upstairs bedroom window flew open and Fuzzy leaned out. 'Er, everything all right, Fuzzy?' Stan called up. Fuzzy replied calmly, 'Joey will be right down, officers.' Fuzzy then threw his brother out of the bedroom window into the flowerbeds below. The stunned officers thanked Fuzzy for his help and took Joey off to custody via the local hospital.

A builder's yard in Lye was suffering from a series of night-time thefts. Due to this an enthusiastic PC volunteered himself and his despondent mate, Jim, to do some observations on the yard. The plan was to lie low in a caravan within the builder's yard and simply wait for the villains to come. Unlike his colleague, Jim wasn't interested in the results, only the overtime cheque at the end of it. His main concern was to make himself as comfortable as possible and to try and sleep. After only five minutes sitting in the caravan, Jim crawled into his large military surplus sleeping bag, pulling the drawstring tight. Only his nose was visible beneath the hood. Soon Jim was snoring heavily and looking like a fat green maggot.

Two hours later, Jim's colleague saw three

men cut the chain-link fence and enter the yard. Excited, he shook Jim awake as he watched the intruders go to some oil drums and begin rolling them to the hole in the fence. The PC then shouted, 'Now Jim, now!' and raced out of the caravan. He grabbed two of the males and held them as they struggled to get away. 'I'm all right here, Jim, you get the other one,' he shouted back. But there was no sign of Jim. A few seconds later, a large green shape emerged from the caravan. The maggot-like shape hopped across the yard after the third villain. Strangely enough, Jim was unable to catch him.

Learning that Jim was shortly off to the USA for his holidays, the rest of his police station decided to set him up. In the months leading up to the trip, Jim constantly pestered them for any bits of kit, cap-badges, truncheons, etc., that he could swap with the police in America. The last time Jim had been to America, loads of cap badges and bits of kit had gone missing from the police station. Everyone knew it was down to Jim but no one could prove it. It was decided that one of them would lose a cap-badge. All were in on the wind-up, including the inspector.

The inspector called everyone into the parade room and explained that the thefts of kit had to stop. He then mentioned that in the last few days yet another cap-badge had gone. This particular cap-badge, however, had the collar number of its owner scratched on the back. The inspector ordered all officers to remove their cap-badges. Jim's colleagues had, of course, engraved on the back of Jim's cap-badge the collar number of the supposedly stolen badge. Jim pulled the badge from his hat with the confidence of innocence and slowly turned it in his hand, whereupon the colour visibly drained from his face. The inspector asked, 'You okay, Jim?' as Jim was now swaying on his feet. 'I've been stitched up, boss,' Jim replied, dropping the badge to the floor. 'In my office NOW you thieving bastard,' roared the inspector. For some reason no more kit went missing after this.

A celebrated West Midlands detective, who had been in trouble off and on throughout his service, was summoned to see the new chief constable for yet another bollocking. The DC had never sat his promotion exams, which was a good thing as he enjoyed life at the sharp end too much. The new chief, lashing into him with a 20-minute tirade of abuse, told the detective that he was very lucky not to lose his job. Red in the face with anger, the chief finally said, 'Right, I've said my piece. Is there anything you want to say, Detective Constable?' The DC, who was only six months away from his retirement, paused for a moment as if thinking and said, 'Yes sir. Will this adversely affect my promotion prospects?'

One day a superintendent received an impertinent memo from an officer at his station that sent him into a blind rage. The memo was signed but the superintendent didn't know who had written it. He sent it out to the different shifts, demanding to know whose signature was on the memo. The memo finally ended up back on his desk with the following additions: 'Sir, A shift, no knowledge. B shift, no knowledge. C shift, no knowledge. D shift, no knowledge. CID, no knowledge.' Someone then penned the following. 'Sir, this memo has been passed to all departments and nobody can identify the signature.' This was then signed with the same signature that had caused all the commotion.

During the miners' dispute, when police got pelted for hours with stones, sticks and copies of *Pigeon Fanciers Weekly,* it was decided that officers would launch occasional sorties into the crowd to try and push them back. One of the West Midlands divisions, from Walsall, was especially keen on this tactic and was making rush after rush into the crowd. It became obvious after a while that the PCs were actually doing this on their own initiative and that their inspector, who was a typical little ginger-haired wimp, had totally lost control. The inspector managed to get around to the front of his unit in a vain attempt to gain control, and with his back to the miners, shouted, 'I am in command here, if any of you break ranks again without my direct order I will put you on a charge.' Someone in the Walsall ranks shouted, 'He said "charge"', at which the entire unit then screamed 'CHARGE!' and ran forward, right over their own unfortunate inspector.

A drunken 24-year-old Swedish male was arrested for slapping a woman before running out of the pub into the street, where he had verbally abused a passing police unit. The male was put in the back of a police car by two PCs and their portly

sergeant and taken to custody. En route the
conversation went as follows:

Sgt: 'Right then, mate, what's your
name?'
Detainee: 'F*ck off you fat c***.'
Sgt: 'That's not very nice.'
Detainee: 'F*ck off you fat f*ck.
Don't speak to me. You are beneath
me.'
Sgt: 'You're not English, are you?'
Detainee: 'You are very perceptive
for a fat useless f*cking lowlife cop.
No I am not English, thank God. The
English are f*cking inferior.'
Sgt: 'Are we really? So, where are you
from then, mate?'
Detainee: 'I'm from Sweden you fat
c***. And I am not your mate.'
Sgt: 'Sweden, eh? So then, mate,
what's your name?'
Detainee: 'I'm not telling you my
f*cking name. You are inferior to me,
you stupid fat c***.'
Sgt: 'In that case, sir, I shall name
you Lager Lagersson, for it has a
certain ring.'
Detainee: 'F*ck off you fat c***. You

27

are really fat, do you know that?'

Sgt: 'Yes, Lager Lagersson, I suppose I could lose some weight. I am working on it, Lager.'

Detainee: 'Don't call me that.'

Sgt: 'Call you what, Lager Lagersson?'

Detainee: 'Lager Lagersson. It's not my name, you c***.'

Sgt: 'Yes it is. Your name is Lager Lagersson.'

Detainee: 'Don't call me that, you fat c***. You are all f*cking arseholes. You are f*cking beneath me.'

Sgt: 'Whatever you say, Lager Lagersson.'

Detainee: 'That's not my f*cking name!'

On arrival the Swedish male and his escort waited in the holding area for the custody sergeant to become available. Lager Lagersson, meanwhile, began to abuse all persons present, including another, well-known, prisoner. He then accused everyone of being Nazis and stated that Germany had in fact won the war. One of the PCs went to warn the custody sergeant of the Swede's manner, suggesting he be put straight into a cell. The custody sergeant, however, who was an incredibly patient and passive man, refused to do this, convinced that he would be able to calm the prisoner down with his verbal judo, as he put it. The PC then went back into the holding bay, where he found the other prisoner, now being restrained, demanding, 'Give me five minutes alone with this guy. I'll show him who won the war.' Thinking that they'd like to, the sergeant and his two PCs quickly whisked the abusive Swede out of the holding bay and stood him in front of the custody sergeant, who smiled welcomingly and said, 'Hello, I'm the custody sergeant and am here to look after your welfare. Can you tell me your name, please?' 'My name is Lager Lagersson, you f*cking c***!' screamed the Swede. 'Throw Mr Lagersson straight into a cell!' bellowed the custody sergeant. 'With pleasure,' replied the escorts.

PC Wright lived with his wife in Milton Keynes, choosing to commute down to London every week for his shifts. In the parade room one morning after his weekend off he told the following story to his colleagues: 'You're not going to believe this. I got home a few hours early on Friday and found an intruder in my house. A f*cking burglar.' 'Blimey! What happened?' his colleagues asked. 'Well, in I walked to see some f*cking bloke hot-tailing it out my bedroom window. Wish I'd caught the bugger.' 'Did he take anything?' the others asked. 'No, thank God. I disturbed him in the nick of time.' 'That's all you need on your weekend off,' a colleague remarked. 'Where was your wife in all this?' 'Well, that's it, see, she was downstairs on the couch wearing next to nothing. Thank God I got home when I did or who knows what might have happened.' PC Wright then left the room after which the rest of the relief exchanged knowing looks. The sergeant summed things up nicely:

'Burglar, my arse.'

Off-duty PC Brennan was out for the evening in Woking town centre with his brother, Danny. At about 1 a.m. the pair were crossing a car park when they saw an Asian male walking around a red Peugeot, looking in the windows and trying all the door handles. Walking up to the male, PC Brennan said, 'All right mate. Your car, is it?' The male replied, 'Yeah, it is.' 'Oh right, 'PC Brennan said. 'Are you sure?' 'Yeah,' the male said. 'I know my own car.'

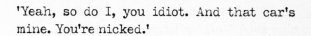

'Yeah, so do I, you idiot. And that car's mine. You're nicked.'

Police were called to attend a report of a knife-wielding intruder committing a burglary. On arrival police saw an agitated male rush out of the premises and, believing him to be the armed intruder, they deliberately ran him over, breaking his leg in the process. The police officers then got out and approached the male, who was screaming in agony on the floor. 'Call me an ambulance,' the man shouted, to which one of the officers replied, 'You're an ambulance.' The officers' laughter soon stopped when it became it apparent that the man on the floor was in fact the burglary victim.

A PC and his sergeant attended a recent domestic burglary. Searching the garden, they found muddy footprints leading into the house from the lounge window. They then went to the kitchen to check the back garden for the thieves' exit point. On entering the house the officers were pestered by two cats that were under their feet the whole time. The PC decided to open the back door and both cats happily shot off up the garden through the flowerbeds, rolling in the wet grass. Police found no signs of the offender or any discarded property, so they came back into the house and shut the door, leaving the cats to play in the garden. The house owner then arrived and was asked if there was anything of special interest in the house that might have been taken, as nothing appeared to be missing. 'No,' said the house owner, 'the only thing in this house worth any money are my two pedigree cats. They are both worth about £1,000 each.' 'Wow!' the PC said, 'I bet you hate them getting dirty, then.' 'That's not a problem,' she replied, 'I never let them go outside.' The PC's heart sank, while his sergeant tried to conceal his laughter. The PC then casually walked to the kitchen, and out the back door to retrieve the two now very muddy pedigree show cats that the burglar must have allowed to escape.

A Cornish detective inspector with Surrey Police was finally given time off after a hectic murder investigation. An hour into the train journey he woke up after having one too many whiskies and asked the guard what time the train arrived in Cornwall. The guard replied, 'It doesn't, this train is going to Cardiff.'

Met PC Bob Warren was on foot patrol one lonely night and was walking along the rear of the shopping parade when he heard a noise in a shop yard. With truncheon in one hand and torch in the other he darted into the yard. His foot struck a soft heavy object and, looking down, in the light of his torch he saw the severed head of a woman lying on his foot. Jumping to one side his foot struck yet another head. Its dull lifeless eyes looked up at him through wet bedraggled hair. He pulled out his whistle, placing it to his lips, and blew like mad to summon assistance to the scene of carnage. Some seconds later it dawned on him that he was in the yard of a ladies' hairdresser.

PC Jon Suave received a report that somebody had deliberately shaved the back legs of an elderly lady's beloved black cat. PC Jon Suave thought it best to attend the address in Farnham, Surrey, as the victim was quite distraught. At the house, the lady told him that she believed the culprit to be a local lad, well known to police, whom she thought was also disqualified from driving. She went on to say that the lad was regularly speeding around the estate and flouting his ban. PC Jon Suave, recognising the lad as an up-and-coming crook, started to tap her for information, sensing an opportunity to make a good arrest. He told the lady that, unfortunately, there was no direct evidence to prove the lad was responsible for the wicked deed to her pet. In an effort to reassure her, he added, 'Still, there's more than one way to skin a ...' Fortunately, he managed to stop himself.

Two Surrey PCs were ordered to meet up with their sergeant at a local railway station one night duty after they had failed to listen and respond to his numerous radio messages. The sergeant pulled up in his car alongside the officers' vehicle and proceeded to give them a right old bollocking, lasting around ten minutes, about radio procedure and the need to keep in touch for officer safety reasons. The sergeant eventually finished his bollocking with the sentence, 'It may be only pieces of metal and wire, but that radio could save your life.' He then reversed straight into a concrete bollard. One of the officers leaned out of his window and said to his embarrassed sergeant, 'It may only be a metal shell, Sarge, but that car could

save your life.' The only sound heard from
the sergeant as he examined the extensive
damage to his vehicle was something very
similar to 'duck off'.

Thieves thought they had hit the jackpot
when they burgled a house and found a pot on
the mantelpiece marked 'Charlie', a slang
term for cocaine. They gleefully snorted the
powder as they ransacked the house in search
of valuable items to finance their drug
addictions. It was only later, after arrest, that
they learnt to their horror that the pot had in
actual fact contained the ashes of the
occupant's dead dog, called Charlie.

Superintendent George Sutcliffe had one pet
hate, and that was coppers who tried to work
the system. Woe betide anyone who tried to
pull the wool over his eyes. His displeasure
can therefore be imagined when he checked
the station sick records, and found that a
certain PC had been taking a lot of
uncertified sick leave. Just the odd day here,
the odd two days there. It didn't take the
superintendent long to put two and two
together. All the PC's absences coincided with
events on the local sporting and social

calendar, or dates when he had been detailed for particularly onerous duties. He therefore wasted no time in summoning the unfortunate PC to his office, and giving him a jumbo-sized bollocking. He told the officer he was aware of his little game, and held back nothing of his opinion of skivers and shirkers. The PC, taken aback by this verbal assault, and unable to get a word in, settled for giving a fairly good imitation of a goldfish. When he had exhausted the topic of the PC's sick record, Superintendent Sutcliffe changed tack and launched another barrage. 'That's not all,' he bellowed, 'I've checked the custody and process records for the past six months! No sign of your bloody name anywhere! When was the last time you locked anybody up, or reported them for summons?' Not the brightest of chaps, the PC thought he saw a light at the end of this tunnel. Managing to interrupt the superintendent, he said in his defence, 'That can be explained, sir. You see, I've been off sick a lot recently.' It is rumoured that the mechanics in the police garage, two floors below and over two hundred feet away, heard the superintendent's scream of fury.

Some years ago, in the days before radios, PC Waller was on duty in the town centre outside the local pictures when he saw the cinema delivery lorry having some difficulty reversing out onto the main road. Going to the driver's aid, he stopped the traffic and helped the lorry reverse out and drive off. Soon after, a bell started ringing on the nearby police phone box, and PC Waller, feeling pleased with himself, strolled over and answered it. 'Keep your eye out for the lorry that delivers the films at the Odeon,' his sergeant said. 'Someone's just nicked it.'

PC Adam Cox was on duty one sleepy afternoon at Trinity Road Police Station when an elderly Irish gentleman by the name of Patrick came into the front office to report a theft. The conversation went as follows:

PC Cox: 'I understand you have had something stolen.'
Patrick: 'Yes. I was in the cafe around the corner having a cuppa when this bloke approached me and said, "Would you like to buy some fags? They're knocked off and going

cheap." Well, I'm an old man, so a chance to save some money was one I couldn't turn down.'

PC Cox: 'What did he mean "knocked off"?'

Patrick: 'Oh, stolen. But it happened several days ago, so that's history.'

PC Cox: 'What happened then?'

Patrick: 'Well, I bought several packets off him. I then thought I could do with some more so I gave him £260 and he went into a nearby block of flats, telling me to wait.'

PC Cox: 'How long did you wait?'

Patrick: 'I waited about twenty minutes for my fags but he didn't come back, so I've come hear to get you to go and get the rest of my fags.'

PC Cox: 'Let me get this straight. You paid £260 in return for some stolen cigarettes that you now want me to get for you?'

Patrick: 'Yes.'

PC Cox: 'Okay, let me have a quick word with my sergeant.'

After a short conversation with his sergeant, PC Cox asked Patrick to come into the custody suite, which he did, and once there he arrested him on suspicion of handling stolen goods. Patrick's reply to the caution was: 'Oh shite, I forgot.'

PC Cox was covering the front office at Trinity Road Police Station when a local villain called Joe, having heard the news that cannabis was to be reduced from class B to class C, walked into the station. Believing it to be totally legalised, Joe said, 'I've got this tenth of pot and there's nothing you can do, copper.' On hearing this PC Cox asked Joe to show him the cannabis, which Joe gloatingly did. Smiles turned to tears when PC Cox subsequently explained that this was not yet legislation and promptly arrested him for possession.

Before Wigan Police HQ was largely civilianised, it was home to a number of long-serving bobbies seeing out their time. One such bobby was PC Pilkington who, having recently been on the receiving end of a wind-up, saw his chance to get his revenge on its author, PC Shaw. This opportunity arose one morning when PC Shaw announced to the office in general that the curry he had eaten the previous night was making its presence felt, and that a visit to trap one was called for. As PC Shaw left the room, PC Pilkington watched him walk down the corridor, and enter the toilet. He quickly ran to his desk, grabbed his mug, which he filled with water, and, mug in hand, sneaked into the toilet after PC Shaw. He then threw the mug's icy contents over the closed cubicle door and ran back to his desk, a picture of innocence. Some minutes later, however, PC Shaw returned to the office, dry as a bone, and completely unruffled. Puzzled, PC Pilkington asked casually, 'Have you got rid of that curry then?' 'I bloody nearly didn't make it,' PC Shaw grumbled, 'Some bugger was already in there, and I had to dash up to the third floor before I could find a vacant bog.' Suddenly, PC Pilkington became very thoughtful. His musing was interrupted by the arrival of a panic-stricken typist in the office. 'I'm keeping out of the way,' she gasped. 'The detective superintendent's on the rampage. Some lunatics just thrown water all over him while he was sat on the lavatory.' For the rest of the day, PC Tony Pilkington kept a very low profile.

40

PC Dallas' father was a gamekeeper and as a result he knew most of the tricks of that trade. One night duty, around 2 a.m., a very upset gentleman called at the front counter of Barrhead police station. The gentleman had been involved in a road accident, in which he had knocked down and either killed or seriously injured a deer. Whilst PC Lyons was taking details, his colleague PC Dallas disappeared. Later, when his fellow PCs went out to look for the deer, it was nowhere to be found. Shortly after this, PC Lyons and his crewmate attended a violent domestic at which they arrested a man who repeatedly threatened officers en route back to the station. The man was dragged kicking and spitting into the police station, along the dark corridor to the old cells. The prisoner was still shouting abuse as the PCs finally managed to push him into a cell. As they attempted to shut the door, the man screamed, ran out and threw himself onto the floor in a foetal position, crying like a baby. Puzzled at his sudden transformation, the officers looked round the corner into the partially lit cell, where they saw a skinned carcass hanging from the ceiling, dripping a huge pool of blood onto the floor. After their initial shock the PCs realised it was the missing deer from the earlier incident. The sobbing male then apologised for his earlier behaviour and for the rest of the night was as quiet as a mouse.

A few years ago, an old PC called Stan Haycocks was attending his leaving do at a local rugby club. There was a massive turnout because Stan was very popular. One old chap, who looked about a hundred odd, was hobbling around in a Zimmer frame. Stan's speech was going well and he introduced the old chap in the walking frame as his first inspector from thirty years earlier. He then moved on to talk about the old days and how he and his fellow PCs used to play cricket in the front office. On one occasion, Stan related, he had smashed the station window with a cricket ball. Suddenly the old chap creaked to his feet and shouted, 'I've got you now, Haycocks. I knew it was you. Passing bus throwing up a stone, my arse. I can prove it now: you've admitted it in front of all these witnesses. You all heard it. He admitted it.' Stan and all present got the distinct impression that the broken window from thirty years earlier had been playing on the old inspector's mind a bit.

After a good arrest, PC Hill unwisely decided to celebrate down the pub with a fellow officer. He was due to work an early shift the next day, while his colleague had a more preferable late shift. A few drinks quickly developed into a skinful and after falling out of a nearby curry house, PC Hill and his mate staggered home, crashing out at the latter's flat. The next morning, an acutely hung-over PC Hill, dressed only in last night's boxers, dragged himself to the kitchen for a drink of water. Just then he felt the desperate urge to fart violently. As he let rip, a classic case of 'following through' resulted, leaving the PC standing in his own shit in his friend's kitchen. Without thinking, and in a panic, he grabbed the nearest thing he could to clean himself, up which just happened to be his mate's freshly ironed, crisp white police shirts. Already late for duty, he stuffed the soiled shirts into his mate's washing machine and made a speedy exit. Once at work, he phoned his colleague, who was still in bed, telling him to get up, go to the kitchen and switch on the washing machine. On no account, PC Hill stressed, was his mate to look into the washing machine. A few minutes later his mate called back to tell PC Hill that he was a dead man. PC Hill was later heard to remark, 'Well, I told him not to look in the washing machine.'

One Christmas Eve, a frantic radio message was received from PC Dave Riley of Kent Police. The message went something like this: 'Priority, priority! Two hundred people fighting at the end of Weak Street. Assistance required!' This had the potential to be a major incident, so numerous police units started to head towards the scene. Seconds later, however, Dave called over the air: 'Cancel, cancel. Situation over.' Now, two hundred people don't just stop fighting, so Dave's sergeant decided to call up to say they would still head towards his current location, just in case. Dave again tried to cancel the units insisting that there was no longer a problem. Thinking that Dave was unable to speak freely, Dave's sergeant declared over the radio that they would not cancel unless he told them why. Not so frantically, Dave sheepishly explained that the two hundred people he thought were fighting were not. In actual fact, they had just come out of midnight Mass and had been enthusiastically hugging and kissing each other to say Merry Christmas.

A dog handler, PC Alan Jameson, of Barnsley Police, had a scheme involving a local school called Adopt A Police Dog, whereby the handler went to local schools and told them tales about police dogs. In return, PC Jameson was allowed to use the school, when closed, for training his dogs. The dog handler also took with him guest speakers such as traffic officers or mounted branch to give the kids an insight into the job and promote public relations. On one such occasion, he took with him one PC Kaczmarczyk, who was the local wildlife officer and who was also a keen falconer. PC Jameson thought it would be a good idea if PC Kaczmarczyk took his hawk along and did a small display for the kids. The dog handler went through his normal routine, meeting the kids in the assembly hall with his dogs and after a short talk introduced the local wildlife officer. PC Kaczmarczyk immediately went into his routine about the beauty of the countryside and the dangers of climbing trees, playing near rivers, and closing gates. He told the children that under no circumstances must they endanger the lives of animals, take eggs from nests or shoot birds. PC Kaczmarczyk then left the hall and returned with his Harris Hawk. The kids' faces lit up with excitement and, as the bird stretched its wings, the room was full of 'Oohs' and 'Aahs'. It was then decided that the whole school would go outside for a display, which would consist of PC Jameson running up the field, dragging behind him a lure for the hawk to swoop on.

The kids were all lined up in the field and PC Kaczmarczyk released the hawk, which circled and then flew into a nearby tree. This was normal practice, PC Kaczmarczyk assured the crowd, before recalling the bird to his arm. He then allowed the hawk to fly again. This time the hawk flew straight onto the school roof. PC Kaczmarczyk tried numerous times to get the hawk back, but the bird was having none of it, much to the delight of the school kids. The hawk then suddenly looked up and saw a passing pigeon, and in an instant flew at it, caught it and pulled its head off. The kids' delight quickly turned to anguish and laughter was replaced by screams and wailing as the pigeon fell to earth minus its head. The hawk then flew over a nearby hill and out of sight.

PC Kaczmarczyk went running off in search of his beloved bird, while PC Jameson was left to entertain and console the kids. After ten minutes or so, the wildlife officer returned with his hawk and an irate local pigeon fancier, the hawk having killed his prized racing pigeon. After some negotiation, the pigeon fancier was pacified with a handful of the green stuff. Not to be outdone, PC Kaczmarczyk, decided to continue with the display. The kids' spirits were again raised as the show resumed. PC Jameson was then given a go at running up the field with the lure. 'What do you use for the lure?' PC Jameson asked, at which PC Kaczmarczyk pulled from his pockets a handful of lovely yellow dead chicks. Those poor kids!

Following a report that youths were breaking into a car, PC Garland from Whitefield, Greater Manchester, who was working in plain clothes, donned his baseball cap, ran out of the police station and, in an unmarked car, rushed to cut the offenders off. He explained over the radio that he was covert and asked that patrols keep out of the area. Making his way down the streets safe in the knowledge that no one would suspect that he was a cop, PC Garland was surprised when a passing local councillor wound down the window of her car and said, 'They've gone that way, officer,' pointing down a back alley. Perplexed that he had been sussed, he supposed his radio must have blown his cover. There was no trace of the youths and resuming his patrol he took off his baseball cap ... a black baseball hat with a nice bright chequered band running around it and the word 'POLICE' emblazoned on the front. Looking across he saw his other - Nike - baseball cap lying on the seat. He was later quoted as saying, 'I felt like a right twat.' No one disagreed.

In February 1983, Met PC Pete Tyrrel was based at Muswell Hill and was starting night duty when Denis Nilsen, the now infamous serial killer, was arrested for a series of murders of male guests he had invited back to his flat. The following night, PC Tyrrel was instructed to guard the crime scene at 23 Cranley Gardens, the attic flat where Nilsen, had murdered young males and cut up their bodies for disposal in his garden and down the drains. PC Tyrrel was given the choice of either sitting in the downstairs flat or standing in the hallway at the front door, which was left partially open to allow the pungent smell from the house to escape. For reasons of warmth, PC Tyrrel chose to sit inside the flat. The only lights working were those in the ground floor rear sitting room;

both the hallway and stairs leading to the attic flat were in complete darkness. From the road outside, the house was not showing any lights at all. There was an old gas fire in the rear sitting room, which was on full blast, and PC Tyrrel crouched over this to keep warm. From where he sat he could see the stairs disappearing into the blackness leading to Nilsen's flat.

At around 3 a.m. the exceedingly jumpy PC began to hear voices from the road outside getting louder as they approached the house. The voices were both male and female and their owners were quite obviously the worse for drink. PC Tyrrel quietly decided to investigate. Through the open front door he saw two young couples by the front gate. Standing in the dark, the PC heard one voice say, 'I dare you to go in, look, the door's open.' One of the males looked up and down the street then, and, staggering slightly, walked slowly up to the front door, his friends egging him on as pushed the door wider open. PC Tyrrel let him put one foot into the hall then, from out of the darkness, he said in his best Exorcist voice, 'I am the Devil!' It came out louder than intended and seemed to reverberate all round the house. The drunken male screamed, fell back from the door and, sobbing in fright, tore off down the path, his friends at the gate already running up the road screaming for all they were worth, the girls' high heels clattering as they ran. Later, PC Tyrrel was heard to remark, 'I'd love to know what they said to each other when they finished running. One thing's for sure, I certainly wouldn't want to be doing their laundry.'

PC Pearson was covering Leeds city centre as a van driver with his colleague, Nick. Their early start brought them onto Inspector Mills shift. Mills was an old school inspector whose word was law and for whom the words 'no' and 'can't' did not exist. Unlike office-bound inspectors of today, Mills often went out alone in the city centre, patrolling his domain, as he was this very evening. Now, PC Pearson's first job of the night was to transport a stray mongrel from the police kennels to the RSPCA centre. The dog, a mangy, sad-looking stray, was put in the back of the their van and the PCs drove out of the yard.

Almost immediately their nostrils were assailed by the most noxious stench imaginable. The PCs gave each other accusing looks before glancing back into the rear of the van, where their passenger had just crapped all over the seats. On further inspection, the PCs noticed this wasn't just any old kind of crap, but the canine equivalent of diarrhoea: yellow, runny and stinking. The PCs were forced to drive with their heads out the window as they headed at some speed towards the RSPCA centre. It was at this point that a royal summons came over the radio from Inspector Mills: 'I want the van to head to Boar Lane to pick up a drunk.' PC Pearson desperately tried to explain that they were committed over the radio, but 'No buts', came the reply over the air, 'I want the van now.' The PCs soon arrived at the inspector's location, where they found him holding an innocuous five-foot-nothing male, clearly the worse for drink, by the scruff of the neck. Opening the van's rear doors, the inspector visibly recoiled, his moustache and nostrils twitching at the foul stench from within. 'What the f*ck is that?' he exclaimed. 'We tried to tell you sir ' attempted PC Pearson. 'Well, you didn't try hard enough!' Mills boomed, and without further ado dragged out the luckless mongrel and sent it on its way, divisional dog lead still attached, with a badly aimed kick. 'Damn,' he barked, 'the f*cker's escaped.' The inspector then threw his hapless drunk into the rear of the van, right across the soiled seats, where the poor man lay sprawled, and slammed the doors shut. He then ordered, 'Take him to Detox and get him checked out.' The PCs, knowing full well that Detox would not accept their pitiful shit-covered cargo in his present state, thought quickly. 'We're going to have to hose the van out anyway, so let's take him back to the nick and hose him down as well,' Nick said. It seemed like a good idea, so back to the station they went.

In the yard the PCs propped the man against the wall and washed him down with the fire hose before hosing down the van's interior. Fortunately for the drunk, it was a mild summer's evening. Having sprayed the van with air freshener they then put the drunk back in the van and set off again for Detox. On arrival the PCs hauled the drunk into reception, where he stood dripping copious amounts of water onto the carpet. 'What the hell's happened to him?' asked the receptionist. Ever the quick thinker, Nick replied, 'Er, he fell in the river, love.' Now, the River Aire at that time was a filthy brown open sewer polluted with every type of natural and chemical effluent known to man. 'Well, we can't take him then, you'll have to take him to the Leeds General Infirmary for a check-up, came the reply, and the PCs were ushered out. 'Well, we're committed now,' said Nick, so off they drove to Casualty.

Nick repeated the story about the river to the nurse in Casualty and the drunk was wheeled off on a trolley to undergo the further uncomfortable indignity of a stomach pump. As if this wasn't enough, the drunk then suffered the added pain and humiliation of having his trousers pulled down and a series of injections against everything from the bubonic plague to God knows what administered to his buttocks. He was handed back to the custody of the two PCs, who finally returned to Detox where the poor sod was left to sleep the whole thing off. It is not known whether the drunk ever returned to Leeds city centre, but certainly the PCs never encountered him there again.

In the 1960s, following a spate of thefts of knickers from washing lines, PC Daniel

Goldsmith was in plain clothes one night carrying out observations in the Norwich Road area of Lowestoft. This particular night was dark, cold and foggy and after some hours pounding the streets PC Goldsmith's craving for a fag got the better of him. Finding a suitable spot on a garden wall with a chain-link fence to the rear, he sat down and, placing his torch between his legs, got out his tin of trusty Old Holborn and began to roll a cigarette. Suddenly, the PC heard the chain fence clinking and felt hot breath on the back of his neck. He turned to see a ghastly white figure with horrible yellow eyes standing immediately behind him. Jumping up in terror, the PC abandoned his torch and, scattering his tin of tobacco across the pavement, bolted back down the alley, wailing in a blind panic. Reaching the relative safety of the street lamps he finally stopped and caught his breath, reflecting on the hideous demonic apparition that he had just witnessed. Eventually, the need for a cigarette overcame his fear and he decided, against his instincts, to return and retrieve the torch and tobacco. Creeping back into the darkness, he made his way to where he had been sitting and finally located the torch. With truncheon drawn, the PC then shone it back towards the chain-link fence, where its beam illuminated the terrifying figure of an old billy goat standing with its front feet draped over the fence.

An unsuccessful robber, who had spent most of his adult life inside, decided to pull off the Big One, the job that was going to set him up for life. This was not the best course of action, given that an informant was leaking his every move to DS John O'Connor, a rural Kent detective, who quickly learned that the robber's intention was to rob the local post office. According to his snout, the blag would take place on a Wednesday (the day before pensions were handed out, when the office would be stuffed with cash). Detectives therefore watched and waited patiently for three weeks every Wednesday, but the robber never showed. The following Tuesday, however, two armed men wearing crash helmets entered the store and demanded money. The postmistress handed over a bag of pre-marked cash, which police had provided, and triggered the alarm. In a panic, the robber grabbed the cash and he and his mate fled towards their getaway car, which was a clapped-out Mini. A member of the public witnessed their exit, however, and heroically decided to follow in his new 4x4 while also putting a call in to the law on his mobile phone.

The driver maintained a commentary to police as he drove after the Mini, which eventually crashed in a field. Unhurt, the robbers ran off in different directions and the public-spirited motorist ran after the robber with the swag bag. Unfortunately for the robber, this motorist happened to be an experienced marathon runner while he, weighed down by his years of porridge, was not. Exhausted, the robber finally turned to his pursuer, and pulling off his crash helmet gasped, 'Here, take the money but let me go, mate.' 'Hello Keith!' said the driver, 'Weren't we at school together?' 'Oh shit.' The robber was soon arrested. His accomplice was later found hiding in a tree near the crash and also arrested.

'Never heard of him in me life!' the robber stated in interview when the name of the other man was put to him. His bravado was short lived after a photograph found by police in his flat was shown to him. It was the robber and his accomplice sitting with arms around each other's shoulders, sharing a prison cell. 'Shit,' was the robber's reply. 'Shit, shit, shit.'

One particularly quiet night shift in a Surrey backwater, when not too much was happening, the airwaves were disturbed by an almighty yawn followed by an anonymous but vaguely familiar voice, which crackled over the radio, 'God I'm bored.' As PCs across the county began chuckling at this transmission an irate inspector stationed in the control room grabbed the mike from the operator and said, 'Who was that? Would the unit who transmitted the last please declare themselves immediately,' to which the voice was heard to answer, 'I said I'm bored, not stupid.'

Surrey PCs Steve Stamp, Simon Quinn and their burly ex-navy sergeant Pete Hogben were conducting a check on some youths at around 1 a.m. in Walton Town. The youths seemed okay and PC Stamp was keen to finish the check and move on to a better stop. All of a sudden a car full of baseball-capped youths drove past in a battered old car, which had a smashed side window. That car's nicked, thought PC Stamp, sensing a good arrest, and ran after it. Desperate to get the attention of his sergeant, he turned as he ran and shouted back, 'Dad!', to the great amusement of all present, who collapsed with laughter as the suspect car disappeared. PC Stamp's close relationship with his sergeant was now fully explained to the rest of the station.

PC Ray Davis of Greenford Police was with his colleague in the early hours of the morning, walking down a poorly lit road by the side of a cemetery, when in front of them they saw a gang of local yobs. The PCs heard the yobs daring each other to go into the local cemetery. Sensing an opportunity, the two officers quickly popped into the cemetery grounds behind a line of trees and caught up with the group. One or two youths finally plucked up the courage and entered the cemetery leaving their mates standing just outside. As the two approached the PCs let rip with as many clichéd groans and sighs as they could without laughing and rustled some bushes. All went quiet for a fraction of a second, then all hell broke loose. The group started screaming at the top of their voices, 'There are f*cking ghosts in here!' There was a long line of hedges at the side of the graveyard and the two youths didn't wait for a gap but ran straight through the hedge and up the road after their already fleeing mates, leaving an outline of their bodies behind them like something out of Scooby Doo. PC Davis later heard that the local yobbery were now convinced that the place was haunted. He and his colleague, however, knew better.

Six South London PCs were called to attend a violent domestic incident. On arrival a distressed female screamed that her husband had just assaulted her and that he was now hiding in the garden. The officers hurriedly went out into the garden, where they found the husband, a tattooed monster who had spent all afternoon down his local pub, lurking on the patio. Seeing the six PCs, the man pushed out his chest and clenched his fists. 'Come on then, you f*ckers, how many of you does it take to nick me?' the man shouted defiantly. At this, PC Phil Long, an old sweat who had just about seen it all, calmly walked up to the man saying, 'Just me, mate.' He slapped the handcuffs on the man's wrists, said, 'You're nicked,' before calmly leading the surprised brute out to the car.

One night just after World War Two, an arsonist used a paraffin lamp to set fire to the front door of a house before running off. Fortunately, a neighbour alerted police in time and DC Gidley attended, calling for a police dog handler to assist him. The dogman and his large Alsatian dog soon arrived and the Alsatian cast around for the paraffin scent track. The dog was definitely onto something, for he was tracking intently. Eventually the now frantic police dog stopped at the door of a house some 400 yards from the crime scene, its tail wagging madly. DC Gidley knocked at the door, which was answered by a lady in a nightgown who explained that her husband was out on shift work. Suspicious, the DC and the dogman decided to search the premises, explaining to the lady that the police dog had followed a track straight to her house following an arson attack. 'Can I stop you there, officers,' said the lady, turning round and giving a shrill whistle. From the kitchen there came running out another large, excited dog. 'This might have something to do with it. This is Suzy, she's an Alsatian bitch and she's on heat.'

PC Gidley and his colleague responded to a report of a man having just broken into a car at around 1 a.m. Driving down Stockton High Street they passed over the filthy River Tees, where they saw a man matching the description circulated standing in the centre of the bridge. Stopping the car they jumped out, but the man suddenly disappeared. PC Gidley then noticed something white on the parapet's edge. Looking over, he saw the same man hanging by his fingertips above a sixty-foot drop to the river below. Grabbing an arm each, the officers roughly hauled him back over the parapet. 'Hey, watch it,' the man retorted angrily, 'I've got a weak heart.'

At around 11 p.m. one cold night, DC Gidley received a report of a girl having been raped at a bus stop about three miles north of Stockton. The victim had got off the bus and had been followed by her assailant, who subjected her to a terrifying ordeal. The girl gave the description of the rapist to DC Gidley, who then circulated it over the radio. Soon after, another DC in an unmarked police car was flagged down by a male on a lonely stretch of road some two miles away from the bus stop, who fitted the description of the rapist. The man asked, 'Can you give me a lift to town?'

The DC readily agreed and gave him a lift straight to Stockton Police Station, where he was interviewed and later charged with rape.

One night in Stockton High Street, a fight developed and one man was hit in the face with a broken beer glass, causing him severe injuries. DC Gidley established the name of the assailant and went to the man's home address at around 1 a.m. A scruffy grey-haired old woman answered the door and the DC asked if the man he wanted to see was in. She said he was and shouted upstairs, at which a thirty-year-old man in a sweat-stained string vest and pants came down and was subsequently questioned. The house was filthy and the DC couldn't wait to get out. Every now and then the suspect would jump up from the chair and stamp with his bare feet on one of the many cockroaches that kept appearing on the floor. The old woman, meanwhile, kept answering the DC's questions on behalf of the suspect, which was becoming irritating. At last, DC Gidley could stand it no more and roughly said, 'Tell your mother to shut up, will you?' The suspect replied, 'That's not my mother, it's the wife.'

PC Ken Evans was on patrol just outside Shrewsbury on his traffic police motorcycle with the hot sun shining above when he came up behind a vehicle that he thought worth a stop. The driver appeared agitated and kept looking nervously back in the rear-view mirror. There was a woman sitting next to him. The PC signalled for the car to pull over, which it did, stopping in a lay-by alongside a fully grown cornfield. Before the PC could dismount, the driver ran off across the cornfield. He went some distance before ducking down out of sight. As it was midsummer, PC Evans, wearing his full leathers, had no desire to run after him. Turning to the woman who was in the car, he asked the driver's name and why he had run. She replied that his name was Elwyn and that he was disqualified from driving.

The PC looked across the cornfield, where the corn heads were fluttering in the breeze. There was no sign of Elwyn. He then shouted, 'Elwyn, if you don't come out I shall release the Alsatian dog.' The PC repeated the threat, saying, 'This is your last chance. Come out or else.' Suddenly, the man stood up approximately 200 yards away, with just the upper part of his torso visible. He raised his arms aloft and shouted, 'Don't let the dog go. I'm coming. The man started to walk towards PC Evans, who thought that at any moment the man would see that he was a traffic police motorcyclist, not a dog handler. The PC held his breath in anticipation, not looking forward to a chase through the corn. Suddenly the man was within range and he grabbed hold of him. 'Where's the dog?' Elwyn asked, to which the PC replied, 'What dog?', slapping on the handcuffs. As Elwyn's girlfriend started to rant about how dumb he was, Elwyn complained, 'What a lousy trick.' He got six months in prison.

The patience of Hampshire's Sgt Thorne and detention officer Ron Macdonald was tested when booking a prisoner into Aldershot custody. Sgt Thorne asked the suspect, 'Have you ever harmed yourself in the past?' The prisoner replied, 'Yes.' 'How?' asked the sergeant, to which the prisoner replied, 'I walked into a brick wall.' The suspect then asked for his friend Kevin to be contacted. The number was duly called but there was no reply. When the suspect was informed he commented, 'There wouldn't be, he's not at home.' The criminal mind never ceases to amaze.

PC 'Crasher' George worked at Clevedon Police Station, North Somerset, and was so called because of his habit of crashing police cars. One day, a faxed copy of a telephone call was forwarded to the police station from the control room. The call related to a complaint made by a good member of the public about the speed of a police car being driven through the town, apparently not for any good reason. Knowing Crasher's driving habits, PC Roger Fry, for a laugh, decided to forge his sergeant's handwriting and wrote the following to his accident-prone colleague: 'PC George, this has got to be you. Please report the reason for the manner of your driving.' Now, when PC George received the note, he went absolutely ballistic, as he was somewhat sensitive when it came to any criticism of his driving. 'OK, he wants a report, I'll give him a report,' he said. PC George then wrote, 'I have been an advanced driver for many, many years. I do not require your permission to travel above 30 mph, and another thing, you're a rotten sergeant and the rota all despise you.'

PC Robinson was on patrol in Sheffield City Centre when he received information over his radio that a male and a female had thrown a brick though a wedding shop window. On arrival he saw that a dog handler had beaten him to the scene and arrested the couple. It was then agreed that PC Robinson transport the female so, ever the gentleman, he opened the police car door for her and told her to get in. As she climbed in she placed her hand on that of PC Robinson, who felt a chilling sensation run through his body as he noticed the size of her hand. Recovering, he said, 'Tell me, madam, are you male or female?' to which she replied 'Sex change, ducky.'

A Surrey PC was in plain clothes and had borrowed the crime unit's unmarked police Astra. As he was driving along the high street he saw a young tearaway walking along the road kicking fences. Parking alongside, he snatched from the dash and put on what he believed to be a stylish Surrey Police baseball cap that members of the crime team often wore. Jumping out, he approached the lad. 'What do you think you're doing? You're going to get yourself arrested. You are very lucky that I'm busy or I'd take you in.' The youth then said, 'How do I know you're a real policeman?' 'What does it say on the cap?' the PC roared, pointing at his head. The lad, ears ringing, apologised and the PC drove off, feeling rather pleased with himself. Glancing in the rear-view mirror, only then did he notice that he was in fact wearing a Royal Mail postman's cap, used by the crime squad as a disguise when executing early morning warrants.

At Tower Bridge Police Station in the mid-seventies, a lazy PC was sleeping on his early shift following a night out on the town. He was hidden away in a windowless cell safe in the knowledge that if any rank appeared a colleague would wake him and give him advance warning. Half an hour before the end of the shift, he was woken up by a friend who told him that the inspector was in the police station and that the he wanted to speak to them all in the briefing room. 'By the way,' his friend said, 'it's been raining heavily all morning.' The PC, in a panic, threw on his helmet and overcoat and rushed to the shower room, where he gave himself a good dowsing before reporting to the parade room soaking wet. As he entered the room he was dazzled by the clear sunlight shining through the window. Looking at his friend, who was smiling broadly, he felt all eyes on him as the inspector shouted, 'In my office now, you lazy bastard.'

A man stole an expensive sheepskin coat belonging to a chief inspector after it was left hanging in the foyer of a hotel hired out for a convention of senior police chiefs. As the thief was walking down the Exeter Road wearing his new sheepskin coat, a coach pulled over and the driver asked if he wanted a lift. The thief readily accepted and jumped aboard quite happy, that is until he realised that it was full of more than 42 senior police officers on their way home. Its owner instantly identified the coat and the man was arrested and taken to the station, where he remarked to the desk sergeant, 'Biggest bloody panda car I've ever seen.'

PCs Steve Murtagh and Maxine Cilia were on patrol in Addlestone Surrey when they received a report of an armed male having taken his parents hostage. PC Piers Hunt called up over the radio saying that he knew the house and would meet PC Murtagh nearby, as he did not believe it safe to go straight to the address. On arrival at the rendezvous point, the two police cars were parked and the officers began to strap on their body armour. All of a sudden a male brandishing a carving knife in each hand came charging out of the very house they were parked outside. The man chased all three PCs round and round the two parked police cars, slashing and lunging at them with the knives. The PCs backed off, at which the male jumped into one of the police vehicles and, to the their horror, started the engine. PC Hunt charged forward and began to smash all the car's windows and several of its panels in an effort to get at the male. The man, however, drove off in the battered police car, leaving the three shaken PCs staring after him down the street. PC Murtagh then turned to PC Hunt and said, 'I hope that's your f*cking car, Piers.'

CHAPTER TWO

TRAFFIC

Traffic officers can be the scourge of many an indignant motorist, not to mention the occasional constable caught speeding to work. It is for this reason that they have aptly been nicknamed the Black Rats by colleagues, due to their well-known habit of eating their own. Having said this, they carry out a thankless but essential role on Britain's roads and the following tales show that they are indeed more human than rodent.

Special Constable Jill Law came across a motorbike displaying L-plates parked in a dangerous position on a busy Essex roundabout. She got out of the police vehicle, marched towards the rider, who was sitting on the grass verge nearby and said, 'Don't you think that's a stupid place to stop?' to which the rider replied, 'I think it's a stupid place to get knocked off my bike.'

In 1953, PC Ewens was involved in a police accident involving a traffic patrol car in which he was the passenger. Such incidents have always been taken very seriously and the driver is usually suspended from driving duties until an investigation is completed. If blame is found, the traffic officer is usually taken off road patrol duties, and may have to move away from the region, with all the associated problems for the PC of moving house and his or her children's school, etc. This particular accident had occurred on a road with a 30 mph speed limit. An opposing lorry had pulled out to pass a stationary vehicle and blocked the traffic car's path. Although both PC Ewens and his driver colleague knew their speed to be 30 mph, or very close to it, their traffic superintendent was adamant that the officers must have been going faster and were therefore partly to blame. The unfortunate driver was suspended and moved to other duties.

Some 28 years later, when both the driver of the patrol car and PC Ewens had retired, PC Ewens was visiting an old colleague in hospital. While there he was informed that the superintendent who had doubted the story about their speed was in one of the beds at the other end of the ward. He had now been retired many years and, after a while, PC Ewens decided to pay him a visit. He reminded the him of the incident in question, which the ex-superintendent remembered well, saying, 'Yes, you both claimed to be only doing 30 miles per hour.' PC Ewens then told him that, in spite of the ex-superindendant's doubt at the time, their speed had genuinely only been in the region of 30 mph. It was obvious that there was no need for any deceit as all parties were now retired and it was all water under the bridge. 'Well I never,' was the ex-superintendent's response.

Three weeks later PC Ewens again went to the hospital to visit his colleague and, while there, he once more went to visit the ex-superintendent. His bed, however, was empty and the patient in the next bed told

73

PC Ewens that he had been discharged. PC Ewens and the patient, whose name was John, then spoke about the superintendent, who had been quite a character and must have been about 80 years of age at the time. PC Ewens mentioned the accident of 1953 and how he had taken the opportunity after all these years to convince the old chap that their speed had only, in fact, been 30 mph. John gave a wry grin and said, 'That's funny, after you left, we were talking and he said that you had spoken about the accident. He then said to me, "Do you know, that young chap is still trying to tell me that they were only doing 30 miles per hour."'

A Merseyside traffic PC was following a large American saloon near the Burtonwood Air base in Liverpool. The vehicle was exceeding the speed limit and failed to give way at a road junction. Sensing a good opportunity to issue a ticket, the PC put on his blue lights to stop the vehicle. The vehicle pulled in and the PC got out and strutted up to the right-hand side of the vehicle, noticing as he approached that there were two American airmen in the car. The airman on that side of the car wound down his window and the PC began to lecture him on obeying the law when a guest in the country and threatened to contact his unit. At the end of the lecture, as the PC took a much-needed lungful of air, the airman said, 'I quite agree with you officer, but shouldn't you be speaking to the driver?' It was a left-hand drive car and the PC had been lecturing the passenger.

PC Cook and some colleagues were on plain-clothes duty on foot in a local town centre, targeting local shoplifters as part of a Christmas campaign. He had recently been suspended from driving duties after being involved in a minor accident, which was now being investigated by the traffic department. The officers, who had not had any luck all afternoon, met outside the local chemist for a final debrief of the day. While most chatted, the eagle-eyed PC Cook noted a suspicious male with goods hidden beneath his coat walking out of the chemist. He started to follow but the thief spotted him and ran. Shouting to his colleagues, he quickly gave chase as the thief began to discard his batteries, razor blades and other goodies down the alleyway.

PC Cook was quick and began to close on the offender, who by this time was reaching the end of the alleyway. At the alley's end there was a road, and against all the best advice given by the Green Cross Code Man, the thief failed to look both ways, running straight out into the road. A vehicle, travelling at around 20 mph, immediately hit the thief, throwing him over the bonnet and over onto the road behind the car.

PC Cook immediately called for an ambulance and gave first aid to the thief, who was not badly injured, but was still shocked and bruised by the events of the chase. He was then arrested and taken to hospital. PC Cook however, was told to stay by the roadside as a traffic unit had been assigned to deal with the accident. The traffic unit duly arrived and, to the amazement of PC Cook, promptly informed him that this was an official police accident and as such a formal report would have to be made to his inspector. Feeling hard done by, PC Cook, asked, 'So what happens now? Am I suspended from running?'

On a quiet night shift, PC Ventham and PC Brennan saw a man driving erratically along

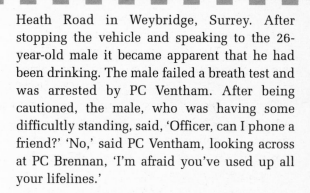

Heath Road in Weybridge, Surrey. After stopping the vehicle and speaking to the 26-year-old male it became apparent that he had been drinking. The male failed a breath test and was arrested by PC Ventham. After being cautioned, the male, who was having some difficultly standing, said, 'Officer, can I phone a friend?' 'No,' said PC Ventham, looking across at PC Brennan, 'I'm afraid you've used up all your lifelines.'

WPC Smith, a Geordie lass working for Kent constabulary and new to the job, was out on her first solo patrol when she came across a French lorry stuck under a railway bridge. Having difficulty making her Geordie accent understood, she radioed the control room for advice and asked for a translation for, 'Can I see your driving documents?' A helpful colleague told her to repeat after him, 'Voulez-vous coucher avec moi ce soir?' The WPC promptly repeated this to the lorry driver, who in turn offered to show her a lot more than just his driving documents.

Sgt Nick Harris was on his traffic police motorbike and following a very dirty white builders' van along the main road through

Farnborough, Hampshire. He followed it for a bit longer then pulled it over. Walking up to the driver, the conversation went as follows:

> **Sgt:** 'I don't believe you have any tax, do you?'
> **Builder:** 'No.'
> **Sgt:** 'I also believe that your MOT has run out.'
> **Builder:** 'Yes, I'm afraid it has.'
> **Sgt:** 'Furthermore, I believe that you have no insurance.'
> **Builder:** 'Yes I have.'
> **Sgt:** 'Are you sure? I have very good reason to believe that you have none.'
> **Builder:** 'OK, I haven't.' (Looking very baffled.) 'Look mate, how did you know all this before you stopped me?'

The sergeant walked him to the back of his van and pointed to the rear doors where, written in the dirt below 'Wash Me' someone had added 'I have no tax, no MOT and no insurance'. The builder's response is actually unprintable, although he did have a driving licence.

A youth, upon reaching his 21st birthday, was given an MG sports car by his father.

Eager to try it out, he got up at 4 a.m. and went to a long, straight stretch of road, where he clocked up over 100 mph. On reaching the village at the end, he reduced his speed before being stopped by the local police patrol. The PC approached the car, and the youth, in a vain attempt of flattery, greeted him with, 'Good Morning, Inspector', to which the PC replied, 'Good Morning, Wing Commander, are you having trouble taking off?'

Two Durham traffic officers were carrying out a routine stop on a heavy goods vehicle. Inside the cab sat the stocky driver and his girlfriend. The driver got out at the invitation of the officers, who inspected the outside of the HGV. The traffic officers then asked the driver to go and get his *chart* out of the vehicle, meaning his tachograph records. A few seconds later, the driver returned with his girlfriend and said, 'What do you want her for?'

Towards pub closing time, two traffic PCs were parked outside a local workingman's club in Surrey, itching to catch a drink driver, when they saw a man leave the club so drunk he could barely walk. The PCs watched the man stumble around the car park, try his keys in five different vehicles before eventually locating his car, which he almost fell into. They bided their time as the man shuffled about in the driver's seat for several minutes while a number of other patrons left the bar and drove off. Finally the man started his car. The PCs watched him switch his wipers on and off, flick the indicators on, before sounding his horn. The vehicle then moved forward a few inches, reversed a little and then remained stationary for a few more minutes as further cars left. At last the man pulled out of the car park and started to drive slowly down the road, eventually switching on his lights. At this, the PCs, started up their patrol car, pulled the man over and breathalysed him. To their amazement the breathalyser indicated no evidence of the man having consumed any alcohol. Dumbfounded, one of the PCs said, 'I'll have to ask you to accompany me to the police station, it seems this breathalyser equipment must be broken.' Smiling, the man replied, 'I doubt it, officer. Tonight, I'm the dedicated decoy.'

A male walked into his local police station to inform the station sergeant that he would be doing a speed test run in his car to see what it could do and was kindly notifying police as he did not want to be stopped for speeding.

Rumour had it that Greater Manchester PC Bill Dalton had been pounding the beat since Rob Peel was a probationer. Extremely popular with the law-abiding public, he couldn't walk 50 yards without being greeted by at least half a dozen passers-by, and it seemed every other motorist would sound their horn and give him a friendly wave. Unfortunately, PC Dalton was rather short-sighted; however, he was always unfailingly courteous and responded with a wave and a smile. It was a standing joke that one day PC Dalton would actually recognise someone and greet them first.

One morning the PC was hurrying back to the station for his meal break when he saw a very distinctive green Jaguar being driven down the road towards him. There was only one car like it in the district, belonging to a local businessman, an old friend of his. As the car approached, PC Dalton stepped to the pavement's edge and raised a hand in greeting. The driver took a moment or two to react. Finally recognising PC Dalton, he smiled out of the car window and gave the PC a thumbs up. He then turned his attention back to the road, just in time to collide with a rusty old pick-up truck. Fortunately, the man was unhurt. He climbed out of his beloved Jag to see the headlamps fall out, and an ominous puff of steam emerge from the radiator grill. Shaken, he thanked his lucky stars there was a friendly bobby to hand and turned to look for Bill. PC Dalton, however, was now three streets away and nowhere to be seen. As he said later, 'I could see nobody was hurt so I f*cked off sharpish.' PC Bill Dalton hated dealing with accident reports and had a funny feeling that this one would prove trickier than most.

A PC on traffic control duty outside a primary school was approached by a six-year-old boy who, pulling at his trouser leg, pointed at the speed restriction humps in the road and asked, 'Excuse me, what are those?' The PC knelt down and replied, 'They are sleeping policemen.' The child thought for a moment and whispered, 'Do we have to be quiet?'

Some years ago, a PC who patrolled a section of the M74 in Scotland received a call to attend a French lorry, which had broken down on the motorway. The PC was well used to dealing with tourists and as his journey took him past his home address, he popped in to collect his French phrase book. On finding the lorry he parked behind the vehicle and approaching the driver, phrase book in hand, asked in his best French what was wrong. The driver of the lorry, in his best Scottish accent, asked the PC what was wrong. The surprised PC then said, 'We've had a report of a French lorry having broken down.' 'Aye,' replied the driver, pointing to a logo on the cab door that read, 'Tam French of Galston in Ayrshire'. 'Oh,' said the PC, putting his phrase book quickly away.

During a snowstorm, a Greater Manchester PC had just finished his refreshment break and was preparing to leave the safety of his motorway post and go out again into the blizzard. Turning his collar up against the biting cold, the PC waded, almost calf-deep in snow, to his Land Rover. It had just gone 2 a.m., so the PC decided to drive up to the county border and park up with the heater on full blast for the rest of the night. Just then his headlights picked up a figure on the hard shoulder. It was a motorcyclist apparently in need of assistance. The PC parked up behind the motorcycle and approached the rider, who was wearing a helmet supplemented by a long scarf wrapped round the neck that covered most of the leather riding gear to the waist. Despite all that protection the poor lad was shaking from the effects of the freezing wind and swirling snow. All attempts to make each other heard were quickly abandoned and the PC, himself a biking enthusiast, quickly discovered the reason for the biker's predicament. Vainly, he shouted, 'Your carburettor's frozen up, mate.' He then tried to convey this by sign language, but merely received a shrug from the biker. The PC, beginning to fall victim to the elements himself, and with a will to get the lad back on the road, decided to adopt a time-honoured remedy. With numbed fingers and taking twice the normal time, the PC unzipped his flies, and stood, legs apart, against the bike. Thanks to the two pots of tea from an hour earlier, the stream he directed onto the carburettor was as accurate as could be expected given the conditions, though a sudden gust of wind caused a back spray that caused the

PC to swear violently. As the PC adjusted himself, the rider mounted the bike and with a single kick, the engine came to life. The PC then signalled for the biker to move off and finally got back into the warmth of his vehicle.

Ten days later his sergeant handed him a letter, which had been sent to the chief constable. 'You were up near the boundary on that date so it must be about you,' said the sergeant. 'Dear Sir,' it read. 'I must draw your attention to the assistance I received from one of your officers on Sunday last, when my motorcycle froze up on the motorway near Blackstone Moor. His gallant actions enabled me to get home safely on a terrible night when I thought I would probably be found the next day frozen to death. Please convey my thanks to the constable, and tell him that he has a perfect right to be very proud of himself. Yours sincerely, Miss Annabel Jones.'

In the centre of Sheffield some 55 years ago, when the tramcars ran through the city, PC Fletcher manned the junction standing on a raised platform. He was directing traffic when he saw a cyclist approaching. The PC raised his arm and indicated for the cyclist to stop before waving a tramcar to proceed across the junction. The cyclist happened to be a police inspector, newly promoted. He called out, 'Fletcher, don't you know I'm an inspector?' to which Joe Fletcher replied, 'Gas, water or electricity?'

A police patrol stopped an elderly couple driving on the M1 after they were caught speeding. The conversation went as follows:

> **Officer:** 'May I see your driver's licence please? You were doing 98 miles an hour. The speed limit is 70.'
> **Driver:** 'No, I was not!'
> **Wife:** 'He drives like that all the time.'
> **Driver:** 'Shhhh.'
> **Officer:** 'Sir, you were not wearing your seatbelt.'
> **Wife:** 'He never does.'
> **Driver:** 'Shut up, will you?'
> **Officer to wife:** 'Is he always this belligerent?'
> **Wife:** 'No, officer. Only when he's been drinking.'

One year on 1 April, Chief Inspector Ken Bull, in cahoots with the divisional commander, decided to send up the traffic inspector, who was somewhat lacking in a sense of humour. The chief inspector prepared a letter purporting to have been sent by the City Hall Traffic Department, which was marked up for the traffic inspector's attention. The letter was to the effect that one Loof Lirpa, the Finnish Minister of Transport, would be visiting Norwich the following day to study traffic flow at busy roundabouts as the Finnish government were in the process of considering the introduction of round-abouts to Finland. The letter went on to explain that in order to afford the minister an accurate picture of how such roundabouts operate, it had been agreed that for two hours that morning at one particular roundabout in Norwich (the busiest) traffic would have to flow in an anti-clockwise direction, due to the fact that traffic drives on the right in Finland. This letter was sent with the rest of the traffic inspector's correspondence to ensure he received it well before the daily Divisional Heads of Department meeting at 10 a.m.

Later at the meeting, when it came to the point at which the divisional commander invited comments from each head of department, the traffic inspector angrily threw the letter down in disgust, expressed his displeasure at the idiots who had sanctioned such a barmy request and questioned the sanity of the divisional commander who had countersigned the letter. At this the commander could hardly contain himself and told the chief inspector to explain. With a large grin, the latter said, 'Read the minister's name backwards.'

The traffic inspector never really forgave Chief Inspector Bull, although he was probably more annoyed with himself for not noticing that Loof Lirpa is the reverse of 'April Fool'.

In 1953, PC Ewens and his colleague were in a Wolsey patrol car answering an emergency call to a serious road traffic accident. It was a dark, wet evening and PC Ewens was the passenger, his colleague was driving, it should be noted, somewhat too fast for the conditions. As they approached a crossroads on the outskirts of Radstock, travelling at a reckless 75 mph, their car suddenly skidded to the offside, aided no doubt by the almost bald tyres that were usual on patrol cars at that time. PC Ewens' colleague whirled the steering wheel to the right, but too late to prevent the spin and they skidded backwards straight at some speed into another vehicle, the impact knocking its driver unconscious. Both PCs were, fortunately, unhurt and PC Ewens quickly set about applying a dressing to the unconscious male while his colleague called for an ambulance. A few seconds later the male thankfully regained consciousness. Seeing the two PCs, his first words were, 'My God, you guys were here quick.'

CHAPTER THREE

NEW RECRUITS

There is no person to be pitied more than the new probationer constable fresh out of the box and unleashed onto the streets amongst battle-hardened colleagues and hard-nosed villains. Being at the bottom of the food chain, the probationer needs all his/her senses to survive the pitfalls of the street, and more particularly of the police station. For a probationer, it's very much sink or swim, with the emphasis on treading water, as the following tales clearly show.

A young PC had to be advised by his tutor on what not to put in written statements after he wrote the following: 'I was tasked with removing the defendant's footwear as evidence. I correctly sealed and labelled both shoes in separate evidence bags. I noticed they were size 8 top-of-the-range Nike Air Turbo Mk111 cross trainers, which I liked to such an extent I subsequently purchased a pair. They cost me £69.99.' Strangely, the PC never made it through his probation.

One Sunday night, a mature 40-year-old female probationer was on foot in Lincoln town centre. As she walked round to the rear of the shopping centre she came across an unsecured rear door. All was in darkness and she could hear hushed voices coming from inside. Excitedly she called for assistance and every unit began heading towards her location. She then called up to say that she could see torches. By now every unit on the division was on its way. Just then she called up and requested that all units be cancelled. Asked by the radio operator why she had done so, she replied over the air that she had, in fact, walked into the rear fire exit of the local cinema and the figures with torches were the ushers.

During the first few weeks of his career, PC Quinn walked into Walton Police Station one night at ten minutes to two in the morning fully kitted up and ready to begin his tour of duty. Going into the briefing room he could find no sign of his team. Where are they? he thought to himself. Just then he came across a sergeant from another shift. 'What are you doing in at this time, Quinny?' asked the sergeant, looking at him strangely. 'What do you mean?' PC Quinn asked, 'I'm due to start a two-'til-ten shift. Where is everybody?' 'Quinny,' the sergeant responded, smiling, 'two 'til ten is a late shift. Most people come in for a late shift at two in the afternoon.' 'Oh bollocks,' replied PC Quinn, turning and walking straight out of the station.

A twenty-year-old PC called Karl celebrated his last night at police training school in the police bar drinking like it was going out of fashion. He awoke the next morning at 6 a.m. in a strange room unable to remember how he got there. Lying asleep beside him was a female police officer with a face like a boxer's dog. Head throbbing, Karl decided to go back to sleep – with any luck it might just be a bad dream. Rolling over, he glanced down to see a bucket by the bed. Raising his head to look out of the window he saw splatterings of his own vomit on the windowsill. By now he was seriously starting to wonder what had happened the previous night and exactly how much trouble he was in. He then looked down and saw that he had also wet the bed. Thankfully, the troll next to him was still fast asleep. Admitting to bedding the troll would have been bad enough but the shame of wetting the bed was just too much. He had to think of something, fast.

For a moment he considered the option of waking the WPC and trying to pin the blame on her, but the risk of not being believed was too great. All of a sudden his recent training in crime scene preservation kicked in. Carefully getting out of bed he picked up an empty glass and filled it ever so slightly from the tap. He then went back to the bed and placed the glass in the sleeping WPCs hand under the covers. The PC then quietly dressed and left the scene of his crime. A few hours later, curious to find out whether the ruse had worked, he was relieved to see the WPC hanging out her water-soaked bed sheets to dry in the sun.

The sun-dried sheets were then returned to her bed and slept on for the rest of the week with the poor WPC none the wiser.

Inspector Nick Maton was a young probationer PC, stationed at Weymouth in Dorset. On one particular occasion, his day shift was coming to an end; before going home he needed to carry out an urgent last enquiry in the town. All of his colleagues were busy and there were no spare vehicles to borrow. As he didn't have time to walk, he took one of the old Community Beat Officer pedal cycles from the store in the station yard and headed off into town.

All was going well, until he started to cycle along the quay at Weymouth. Anyone who has ever been to Weymouth will know that sunk into the road all along the quay are tram lines, which back then were used twice a day by the boat train on its journey from the main railway station to the ferry terminal. As PC Maton rode along he spied a young boy tugging his mother's sleeve and busily pointing at him. Feeling like the embodiment of the traditional British bobby, he threw the lad a cheery wave. Unfortunately, at that exact moment his front wheel became stuck in the train track and PC Maton disappeared over the handlebars, his helmet rolling to land under a delivery van. The young lad looked shocked as his mother tried hard to suppress her laughter and PC Maton, desperate to redeem some pride, took the opportunity to reinforce what had happened by saying, 'Let that be a lesson to you, don't ride your bike near the tram lines.' PC Maton never took a police pedal cycle out again.

WPC Pathan demonstrated her naivety when she was crewed up with DC Batley. They were searching a house for cannabis after a tip-off that the occupier was growing the illicit drug in his garden. While the DC was speaking with the suspect in the house, WPC Pathan went outside to search the garden. She returned triumphantly with a handful of plants that she had just dug up. DC Batley, on seeing the plants, took his colleague to one side and said, with a sigh, 'They're sprouts.'

An arrogant but well-liked PC living in a communal Surrey police section house was starting to irritate his fellow residents over his successes with the opposite sex. Much to the envy of his housemates, this fine-looking officer seemed to have a different girlfriend every week, all of whom seemed to work for some modelling agency or other. To make matters worse, he continually bragged about his sexual conquests and openly flaunted the girls in the communal television area before going off to his room and getting them to make what can only be described as 'nature's noises'. After many months of this, the other PCs in the section house decided to take matters into their own hands.

The next day the officer returned to the section house with yet another stunning girl he had met in a local nightclub and proudly walked into the lounge to have a chat with the lads before retiring to his room with the young lady. As he sat chatting away with a big smile on his face, two PCs made their excuses and left the lounge. They quickly accessed his room via an unsecured balcony window. Knowing the fine-looking officer had a large collection of hardcore pornographic magazines under his bed, the two PCs quickly went about spreading the magazine centrefolds all over the room, covering every possible surface available before turning off the light and returning to the lounge. They were in time to hear their housemate invite his young lady up to his room for a nightcap. As he left the lounge, walking behind the attractive model, he looked back and gave a knowing smile and wink to the remaining PCs in the lounge, anticipating another notch on the already well-whittled bedpost. The PCs in the lounge waited for what seemed like an eternity before a loud slap was heard, followed by a female voice shouting loudly, 'I've never been so insulted, you filthy pervert!' and the distinct sound of the entrance door to the section house slamming shut. A few moments later a very red- and sore-faced officer returned to the lounge and, to his credit, smiled broadly as he was cheered by his fellow section house PCs.

A young Surrey PC joined the rapid entry team hoping to find some excitement and, in his first job, he was asked to assist with a search warrant at the address of a well-known drug dealer's council flat in Camberley. Plans of the address were produced and a briefing was held. The sergeant decided that because he was a new PC he would have to remain at the back to observe. The time came to execute the warrant and the team dressed up in full riot gear and made their way quickly and silently to the council premises. As the burly sergeant strutted towards the front door, wielding the sledgehammer, the young PC suddenly called out, 'Sarge, Sarge, can I ...' but was told in no uncertain terms to shut up by the rest of the team. The sergeant then began to swing his sledgehammer at the door, at which point the PC again called out to the sergeant. 'Shut that idiot up!' barked the sergeant, who then proceeded to bash the door off its hinges, whereupon all of the team, except the young PC, charged inside. On finding the premises empty, the sergeant finally went over to the young PC and said, 'What was so bloody important?' The PC smiled nervously and replied, 'I've got the front door key.'

Early in his service, a stressed PC Matt Ventham was sent by Sgt Hen Lindsley to carry out house-to-house enquiries in a street in Walton-on-Thames, Surrey, on behalf of his colleague who was off sick. The enquiries related to a burglary that had occurred a week earlier. Knocking on several doors in the vicinity of the attacked premises brought no new leads, so PC Ventham decided to call at the victims' address to update them with the investigation's progress (or lack of it). The door was answered by an overweight couple who invited PC Ventham in. Over a cup of tea he proceeded to give them crime prevention advice and conducted a thorough security check of the premises, checking all the windows and the perimeter of the property. The couple repeatedly mentioned how wonderful it was that the police were still persisting with the burglary investigation.

Some 30 minutes later, as he was leaving, PC Ventham asked the couple why they were so surprised and impressed that the police should still be interested. They replied, 'Well, the burglary happened in 1989 and ten years on you're still trying to solve it.' It was then that PC Ventham realised he was in the wrong road.

Met probationer PC Johns was out patrolling with an ex-forces PC when they were called to a park in Brixton to deal with an explosive device found by a member of the public. On arrival they found a grenade with pin still intact lying on the grass. PC Johns was about to request an explosives officer and cordon off the area as per police procedure, when his partner stopped him. 'Hang on, I'm not waiting out here in the cold. Pick it up and well take it back to the nick ourselves.' The probationer was not happy about this, but thought he'd better do as he was told. Reluctantly, and with the greatest care, he picked up the grenade and they returned to the car.

Driving back to the nick, PC Johns carefully held the grenade out in front off him, absolutely terrified that it might explode. The sweat was pouring off his face when suddenly his colleague slammed on the brakes. The grenade flew out of PC Johns' grasp and landed on the floor. Looking down in horror he saw that the pin had fallen out of the grenade. PC Johns turned white, screamed and covered up his face with his arms. The old sweat, however, calmly reached down and picked up the grenade, intending to return the ornament to his mantelpiece, from whence it first came. 'F*cking hell, your face!' the old sweat laughed, 'You must see the funny side?'

'You bastard,' PC Johns responded faintly. 'Maybe, if I hadn't just pissed down my leg.'

On his first day out of training school, PC Ventham was being introduced to his new team at Walton-on-Thames Police Station. PC Steve Brennan asked him who his tutor was.

On hearing the name, Steve shook his head and told PC Ventham that he had pulled the short straw. 'What do you mean?' PC Ventham asked. 'Well, you're not going to learn much being tutored by the Gurkha,' Steve replied. 'The Gurkha?' said PC Ventham. 'Why's he called the Gurkha?' 'He takes no prisoners,' came the reply.

PC Dave McQueen was crewed up with his old tutor, George, a dinosaur of a copper who was known for his particular dislike of cats. If one ran across the road, George would visibly twitch with disgust and actively steer the car towards it, despite the pleas of his cat-loving crewmate. According to George, cats were vermin and that was that. On patrol the PCs attended the flat of an elderly lady who was reporting problems with local youths. The lady was frail and lonely, her only friend in the world the fat tabby cat busy rubbing itself against George's legs as he sat on the sofa. As the lady disappeared to make a cup of tea, George tried in vain to brush the cat away. The cat, in the meantime, jumped on to the backrest of the sofa and proceeded to walk back and forwards behind George's head with its tail up in the air, purring like an engine. George then surprised PC McQueen by lighting up a cigarette, even though there was no ashtray at hand and no sign that the old lady smoked. He waited until the cat was walking away from him on its patrol along the back of the sofa. George then took a huge toke on the cigarette before poking the glowing end right into the cat's ring piece. The cat wailed and shot out of the room like a missile just as the lady walked in with the tea. She asked what had upset kitty and George innocently replied, 'I think he saw a mouse, love.'

PC Steve Brennan was stumbling back to his room, having spent the evening in the Ashford Police Training School bar, when he struck up a conversation with an attractive blonde WPC outside the female dormitory. The WPC mentioned that she had a tattoo on the top of her left thigh, by her groin. Steve, suddenly an art lover, expressed great interest and happily took off his shirt, showing her his own tattoos. As hoped, she then took him aside and, without so much as a by your leave, dropped her trousers to reveal her own tattoo. A trained observer, he immediately saw that she was not wearing any knickers. After pulling up her trousers, the two were joined by PC Suave. Steve then subtly suggested to Suave that he might like to see her tattoo. The pair disappeared for a few moments and on Suave's return, Steve asked, 'So then, what did you think of the tattoo?' Grinning broadly, Suave replied, 'What tattoo?'

Probationer PC John O'Connor was asked one night by the detective sergeant to assist Folkestone CID with some observations. His excitement was short-lived when he realised he was to sit in the back of an old van and keep watch on some lock-up garages that were continually being broken into on a decidedly dodgy council estate. The vehicle was entirely unsuited for the job - old and totally uncomfortable, chosen precisely because it would blend into the surroundings. It had been fitted it out with some rudimentary facilities: an old car seat in the back, a piece of black curtain covering the back windows and an old quilt cover that smelt as if it had seen service with the dog-section. The PC, in plain clothes, was dropped off and he began

watching the garages. The DS had assured
the PC that his back-up would be close by
and was told to call up on the radio if it all
went pear-shaped.

An hour into the watch, the PC heard the
sound of a car engine; its headlights lit up
the back windows. He quickly called up on
his radio, only to find the battery was
flat. A car door banged shut and footsteps
approached. 'Who's parked this f*cking
thing 'ere?' PC O'Connor froze as the van
door handles were tried. Pushing himself
as low as possible in the seat, and
dragging the quilt cover over himself, he
desperately tried to hide the camera and
radio equipment. With a sharp tug on the
handle the rear doors opened and a face
peered inside. Then a torch. 'Christ! What
the f*ck are you doing?' a startled man
asked PC O'Connor, who pretended he had
just woken up. 'Oh, the missus chucked me
out. I'm just kipping down here.

'This is my parking space, mate,' said the
man. 'Oh, sorry,' said the PC. 'Can you shift
it over there?' the man asked. PC O'Connor
then pretended to search for the keys.
'Sorry, I can't find the key.' He prayed the
man would go away. His heart was thumping

so much he feared the man could hear it. 'Don't worry, mate,' the man said, then, 'Tell you what, why don't you come in and kip down on the sofa? My missus left me a while back, so I know what it's like.' The PC's heart sank but, knowing his radio was dead, he got out and followed the man into the house, not wanting to blow his cover.

'Got some Scotch here if you fancy it,' the man said to him. 'Er, no thanks mate,' PC O'Connor replied, 'got to keep a clear head, know what I mean?' 'Yeah, yeah,' the other replied. The two talked for an hour, the PC desperately trying to work out how to get out of this one. The man then announced that he was turning in and threw the PC a blanket before going upstairs.

PC O'Connor lay in the darkness, imagining the furore that must be going on outside now that he had been missing for over an hour. When at last he heard the man's snores from upstairs, he crept to the back door and out into the cold night air. He didn't stop running until he reached the edge of the estate, where he used a phone box to call the station. 'I think they've stood down,' said the control room operator, 'Hang on.' Eventually she located the DS, who said, 'I'll get one of the lads to drive round and pick you up.' 'We'll pick the van up in the morning.' 'What about the equipment?' asked PC O'Connor. 'It'll be all right down there. You shouldn't stereotype, lad. As you know, there are some nice people on that estate,' replied the DS.

In a large north-east town worked a friendly shift with the usual jokers and hard workers. One day, in waltzed a new face, fresh from university, with unmistakable airs of supremacy. This probationer refused to mix with the rest, stating he would be a sergeant after two years and an inspector after three. He wasn't interested in making friends with the lower ranks. And, oh, he'd heard about these jokers who like to take the mickey out of new starters. The new recruit let it be known that nobody was clever enough to catch him out. What a challenge for the hairy-arsed old PC in the control room.

From then on this PC began monitoring this upstart's every movement and action. The PC soon noticed that at the beginning of each shift the probationer would come into the control room and read all that day's incident logs to familiarise himself with what was going on (very commendable). He would also go to the telex machine and read all the messages. With that, the old PC cunningly composed a telex message and, after a quick phone call to his mate in the adjoining sub-division, made certain arrangements.

A few weeks passed with the PC biding his time until, on looking at the duty sheets for night shift the following week, he noticed that the upstart had been allocated the beat that covered the town's park and lake. The night shift duly arrived, and sure enough at the start of the shift in wandered the upstart to look at the incident logs and telex messages. A quick phone call to the PC's mate and the pre-composed message was sent across. It arrived just as the upstart was reading the telex messages kept at the side of the telex machine. Sure enough, he started to read it as it came in. Very important it looked as well, coming as it did from The Ministry of Agriculture. It was a request for any division with an open expanse of water to do a survey. The Ministry wanted to know how many ducks and drakes existed within these areas, as there was considerable concern regarding the decline in drakes from certain parts of the country.

Parade time came and the probationer was

duly allocated the park beat along with the telex, with instructions to carry out its request at the lake and report back to the control room with the results. The first shift was unusually busy. It was 4 a.m. before the old lad radioed the upstart for an update of the survey, as he wanted to get the reply off before he finished. The reply back was, 'I'm doing it now.'

Never before in the history of this sub-division had so many PCs moved so quickly and so efficiently to one spot. They were not disappointed; what they saw exceeded all expectations. The upstart, in his quest for excellence, realised that the lake had an island where all the ducks roosted. The sight to behold was unbelievable, for there he was for all to see, boots and socks off, trousers rolled, up, wading around the island in the lake with torch going in all directions, trying to count ducks separately from drakes. As the laugh went up, the probationer realised he had been caught out, at which point the shit then hit the proverbial fan, and the old lad was disciplined by the superintendent. Fortunately, the super-intendent was of the old school and gave the old lad a dressing down between the laughter. The upstart, well, he couldn't stand the shame and the constant quacking that followed him everywhere he went and shortly after resigned. Anyway, he wouldn't have made a policeman as long as ducks had feathers.

CHAPTER FOUR

THE PUBLIC

Police work would be easy if it wasn't for the public, whose occasional failure to appreciate the demands and complexity of modern policing can often turn the sanest police officer into a raving lunatic. 'It wasn't like this in Dixon of Dock Green' is the common cry. Well, let's not forget that Dixon was shot dead. We may still have to wear headgear more suited to the Boer War, but the occasional stupidity of our customers makes it all worthwhile.

A victim of crime phoned Kent Police to report a burglary at his flat. The call taker asked if the flat was on the ground floor, to which the victim said, 'Hang on a minute. I'll go out and have a look.' During the same conversation the victim was asked his ethnic origin, to which he replied, 'Unemployed.' When the call taker re-phrased the question, the victim replied, 'Oh sorry, Church of England.'

An elderly woman phoned police, asking the operator, 'Can you help me, as I'm locked out and can't seem to find my keys ... I'll wait outside.'

Metropolitan PC John Corkett was manning the phones one quiet night at Harrow Road Police Station when, at 2 a.m., he received a call from a female with a very strong eastern European accent. The conversation went as follows:

PC Corkett: 'Hello, police station, Harrow Road.'

    Female: 'Is that the police?'
    PC Corkett: 'Yes, what seems to be the problem?'
    Female: 'I have got Draculas next door.'
    PC Corkett: 'Did you say you have got Draculas next door?'

Female: 'Yes, I cannot get to sleep. I am afraid of these Draculas. They are keeping me awake.'

PC Corkett: 'Well, to be honest, Draculas are not normally the sort of thing that the police deal with.'

Female: 'You cannot help me with the Draculas?'

PC Corkett: 'Well not really, but perhaps I can give you some advice?'

Female: 'Yes, yes anything to stop these Draculas troubling me.'

PC Corkett: 'Have you got any garlic?'

Female: 'Yes.'

PC Corkett: 'And do you have a crucifix?'

Female: 'I am a very religious woman, of course I have the crucifix.'

PC Corkett: 'Well, put on the crucifix and try to attach the garlic to your clothing.'

Female: 'And this will stop the Draculas?'

PC Corkett: 'Never been known to fail. Draculas hate garlic and crucifixes.'

Female: 'Please, I am desperate, cannot you send someone?'

PC Corkett felt sorry for the female, who was clearly mentally disturbed, so he assigned patrolling PC Taylor to go and visit her. About 25 minutes later, PC Taylor called up on the radio to say that he had visited the woman and that he had arrested a person for possession of drugs. PC Corkett naturally assumed that PC Taylor was referring to the eastern European woman, who was obviously so high on drugs she'd believed Dracula to be living next door, until PC Taylor explained over the radio that what the woman had been saying in her deep eastern European accent was that there were 'drug dealers' next door. He stated he had gone next door and arrested a male in possession of a large amount of heroin and added that the female was very helpful and even offered to lend him a clove of garlic and a crucifix in case the drug dealers gave him any trouble.

In 1951, PC Cliff Blackford, PC Camber, Sgt Spiers and three other PCs decided to conduct plain-clothes observations on a beauty spot in leafy Surrey. There had been a large number of thefts from unattended vehicles and the officers decided that it was time to catch the culprit in the act. A car was parked with a handbag on the front seat as bait and all officers hid in nearby bushes watching the car. After about 30 minutes a tall man, aged about fifty years and wearing a long mackintosh, arrived pushing a bicycle. He propped his bike against a tree and looked into the car, paying particular attention to the handbag. He looked around nervously and then started to open the car door. All six police officers pounced on him, pinning him to the ground.

When he was questioned, it became obvious that he was not the person they were looking for. Just to be sure, he was asked to turn out his pockets. As he did so he emptied out a large number of sticky used condoms from his pockets onto the ground. When questioned he stated that he took them home, washed them and sold them to his mates at work. Disgusted, PC Blackford told him to pick them up and take them away. As the male walked off PC Camber, noticing that he had left one damaged condom behind, shouted, 'You had better take this one. You might need it for patching.'

An elderly gentleman out walking his dog one evening called Surrey Police, telling the operator, 'There's a courting couple naked in a car at the park entrance. I think they are on drugs … She certainly looks like she's had something.'

Scottish PC Dave MacCrimmon and his colleague were called to a house in Falkirk by social services and the district nurse, as they feared for the safety of the resident, an elderly Polish lady. She hadn't been seen for a few days and wasn't answering her phone. PC MacCrimmon opened the letterbox in order to see if there was the tell-tale smell of death. As he did so, he could hear a very faint voice crying for help. He turned to his colleague and said, 'She's not dead.' After kicking, pushing and shoulder-barging the door it gave in taking half the wall with it and PC MacCrimmon ran inside. As he charged in he saw the frail Polish lady lying face down on the living room floor. Not wishing to scare the lady, he then said in his broad Glasgow accent, 'It's all right love, it's the Polis.' To which she replied, 'Yes, yes, I am Polish.'

The police control room in Sussex received a report from an eccentric elderly female who ran a hostel-type address in Hastings. She wouldn't give any detail to the operator, merely saying it was serious incident and she would tell the police when they got there. PC John Hearn duly attended and was ushered into the front room by the elderly lady. She then offered PC Hearn tea and biscuits, which he politely declined. Asked what the serious incident was, she calmly replied, 'Oh, I found one of my elderly residents tied up in his room.' She sat down, took a sip from her cup of tea and said, 'I think he has been there for some time.' Shocked, PC Hearn replied, 'Where is he now?' To which she replied calmly, 'Don't worry, officer, I've left him tied up for you to see.' There was a short pause as PC Hearn tried to register what she had said. He then managed to persuade her to leave her tea and take him to the man's room. On entering the room, PC Hearn saw the elderly male face down on the bed, hog-tied with a number of ties. The man's eyes were bulging and his face was turning blue, so PC Hearn quickly cut his ties and turned to the elderly owner. Before he had the chance to give her a piece of his mind, she shrugged her shoulders and said, 'Well, I didn't think you would believe me, so I left him tied up. You believe me now, though.'

A local beat PC decided to visit the infants school on a rather run-down estate in order to conduct some much-needed public relations work. As he sat talking to the children, who were around five years old, his radio made a loud crackling noise, surprising the children. One of the children then asked, 'Is that a CB?' The PC replied, 'No. It's a police radio. At the end of it there is a policeman. Does anyone here know where the police station is?' 'Why don't you ask the policeman at the end of the radio? He should know,' replied the child.

PC Gail Morris was on station office duties at Guildford Police Station when a young man came in to report a road traffic accident that he'd been involved in. A new form had recently been introduced to cut down on paperwork in relation to injury road traffic accidents. The form consisted of a list of simple questions in relation to the accident that the injured party was required to answer and then return to their nearest police station. The male handed over the completed form, which PC Morris scanned for any errors. She had to stop herself laughing when she got to the section on the form that read, 'My injuries are ...' to which he had written in bold capitals, 'PAINFUL'.

Detective Hughes returned from Hendon very proud of the fact that he was now to be called Detective. There followed a break-in at a factory on the Holm Thorpe Estate in Surrey, and Detective Constable Hughes was sent to investigate. On arrival at the building, he walked into reception, where a delightful young lady on the reception desk asked him who he was and what he wanted. The DC told her that he needed to talk to the manager who had reported the incident, and gave her his name, a bit pompously, as Detective Hughes. She rang her manager and told him there was a Detective Hughes in reception. The DC then saw her face change and could hear a raised voice at the other end of the phone. The receptionist put the phone down and DC Hughes could see that she was having great difficulty keeping a straight face. Unable to contain herself any longer, she burst out laughing. Eventually she calmed down, and told the DC Hughes, in between giggles, that the manager had told her not to waste his time, that she should have contacted the electrician, for, as she said - in between more laughter - 'He said, "I am not paid for little things like that, it's not my job to see to a defective fuse, but an electrician's."'

An angry male dialled 999 and when put through to the police operator declared, 'My wife has left me and taken the dog ... I want the dog back.'

A shrewd builder became a hero when he decided to have a go after inadvertently stumbling upon an armed robbery on a convenience store in Sunbury-on-Thames. When interviewed by police afterwards about what happened leading up to the incident, he explained, 'I was outside and saw these four blokes in a car all putting on balaclavas ... I thought, Hello, it's not that cold.'

In the early hours of the morning, PCs Finch and Shaw were on patrol when they came across four males breaking into a car. Seeing police, the males made off in a battered Ford Capri and a pursuit ensued. Approaching a flyover bridge, the Capri then proceeded to drive the wrong way down an isolated dual carriage. Then, about half a mile further down, with several police units in hot pursuit, the Capri mounted the footpath before finally rejoining the road. About half a mile further still the Capri decided to do a handbrake turn and headed back along the dual carriageway, causing police to take avoiding action. Eventually the Capri could no longer take the punishment and shed a wheel, which went bounding off into the darkness. By the time PCs Finch and Shaw arrived on the scene, all four males had been arrested by traffic.

The officers then started to wonder about a shadowy figure who was emerging from the bushes. As he got closer, they saw his suit was covered in mud and, intrigued, they asked him what had happened. Pulling the twigs from his hair, the figure told them that he had just lost all his money at the casino in Southend, after which he had made a scene and been thrown out into the street. This had pissed his girlfriend right off. She had then taken his jacket, containing all his credit cards, and driven off in his car, leaving him to walk the 20 miles home. Halfway home, some f*cker in a Capri had nearly run him over knocking him straight into a ditch. The figure said he'd waited until he had thought it was safe before climbing out and had just rubbed himself down when, looking up, he saw the same Capri coming straight at him, this time from the other direction. 'What happened then?' asked the two officers, amazed at the man's misfortune. 'Well, I'd just brushed myself down as best I could,' he said, his voice wavering, 'when I see this f*cking tyre coming towards me.'

Two elderly women phoned 999 stating, 'There is a man with no clothes on at the back of our communal garages. We are going back for another look.'

West Midlands officers PC McQueen and his younger colleague, Dave, attended a house following a report from a female that she had been flashed at. Dave was slightly more refined than the average copper and easily embarrassed. He liked fine wine in preference to lager and in no way found farting amusing, which set him apart from most of his colleagues. Knowing all this, PC McQueen got Dave to take the lead.

Dave took down the woman's statement and eventually came to the point at which the victim had to describe the flasher. Having taken the basic descriptive details, it was essential to find out the man's state of sexual arousal. Blushing, Dave asked, 'Was the man erect?' The lady replied, 'Oh yes, love, he was standing up, he wasn't sitting or anything.' 'No. I don't think you understand, was he ... standing up?' Dave asked pointing to his groin. 'Yes, I've just told you, he was standing up on the other side of the stream.' Dave, becoming quite flustered asked, 'No, what I mean is, was he, you know ...' (pointing at his groin again) '... excited?' 'How do you mean love, like jumping up and down?' asked the woman. PC McQueen then interrupted at last: 'Look, did he have a hard-on, love?' 'Oh yeah,' she replied smiling, 'An absolute beauty!'

One night in the 1950s, PC Boast was on night duty directly opposite Grays Inn Road Police Station in London, and was chatting to a Scottish colleague on the adjoining beat about the forthcoming match between England and Scotland, to be played the following morning. As they were talking, a Scottish fan staggered up to them wearing a kilt and matching tartan scarf, obviously well tanked up. The Scottish fan said, 'How do I get to Wembley? I'm down here for the match.' Before PC Boast could say anything, his Scottish colleague cut in, 'The match is being played down in London, it's not up here.' The chap looked at him bewildered and said, 'What do you mean "up here"?' to which the Scottish PC said, 'Well, we're in Aberdeen, you must have taken the wrong train.' 'Oh shite,' said the chap, 'what am I going to do? I've got all the tickets, the lads'll kill me.' PC Boast, joining in the wind-up, and in his best Scots accent, said, 'Well, you had better get back on that train as soon as you can. You might just make it.' The Scottish PC then whispered to PC Boast, 'This idiot has come all the way up here thinking that he is going to London for the match', and both PCs started laughing. The devastated fan turned to go back to the train station, just in time to see a London Transport bus go past. The fan's verbal response was far from complimentary.

PC John Gilling was on patrol in Sidmouth when he came across a distressed four-year-old child who had lost his mother. After some coaxing, the PC established that the lad lived at 43 Roberts Road. Not recognising this address, PC Gilling thought it best to put the kid in his patrol car and drive him around the town in the hope that the boy would recognise a landmark. For an hour they drove around Sidmouth, the lad perking up as he began to enjoy the ride in a police car. At every street corner, PC Gilling would stop the car and ask, 'Do you live here?' and the child would reply, 'No, that's not it.' Finally the radio burst into life. A young woman had arrived at the counter of Sidmouth police station to report a missing child fitting the description of the boy in PC Gilling's car. Mother and son were soon reunited ... but a mystery remained. 'He kept telling me he lives at 43 Roberts Road,' PC Gillings told the woman, still puzzled. 'He does,' beamed mum. 'In Melbourne, Australia. We're here visiting relatives.'

A passing motorist called police on her mobile phone saying, 'There is a large goat running amok on Carlinford Road and the kids will be coming out of school soon.'

Sgt Richard Ford was on foot patrol one sunny afternoon in Bournemouth, when a woman complained to him that a man had just indecently exposed himself to her from a public convenience and that the offender was still there. Shortly after a male was arrested and taken to the police station, together with the woman as the chief witness. When asked to identify him, however, she replied, 'I can't.' 'What do you mean, you can't?' Sgt Ford asked. 'Well, I wasn't looking at his face,' replied the woman.

Police in Blaydon near Gateshead were called to an address after a woman reported that she could hear intruders in the premises next door and that the occupier was away on holiday. The caller stated that she could hear a drilling noise coming from the upstairs of the empty house. Police attended with the key holder and searched the premises diligently but could find no intruders at the address. When they called round the informant's house to update her, however, the drilling noise was still audible. A second search, this time of the informant's house, eventually identified the source of the noise to be a live vibrator in the caller's bedside cabinet.

Amused operators had to keep from laughing when they took the following call from an elderly lady: 'I'm trapped in this phone box by a big dog ... what's more, it's got its thingy hanging out and I'm scared stiff.'

PC Tony Fuller, now retired and a civilian with Surrey Police, was manning the front office of Walton Police Station when a woman came up to the counter. On seeing PC Fuller she immediately began making signs of the cross, muttering prayers and backing away from him. 'What's wrong with you, madam?' asked Tony, his big bushy eyebrows twitching with irritation. 'Get away from me,' said the woman, 'you're evil. Get away from me.' 'Madam, I have absolutely no idea what you are talking about.' 'Keep away, Beelzebub!' she shouted. Turning red, PC Fuller replied, 'Madam, if I cannot help you then see to it that you remove yourself from this police station. I suggest you go and get medical help.' At this she pointed at the epaulets on PC Fuller's shoulders and shouted, 'Satan!' before rushing out of the station, screaming. The station sergeant quickly appeared, 'What was all that about?' he asked, to which Tony replied, 'It's the collar number again, Sarge. I'll have to start covering these up.' With that, PC 666 Fuller resumed his station duties.

Going to bed one night, a resident noticed people stealing garden furniture from his shed. He phoned the police but was told there was no police unit immediately available. The police operator said they would send someone over as soon as possible. The resident then hung up. A minute later, he rang again. 'Hello,' he said. 'I called you a minute ago because there were people in my shed. You don't have to hurry now because I've shot them.' Within minutes there were half a dozen police cars in the area, plus a helicopter and an armed response unit. Police caught the burglars red-handed. One of the officers then said to the caller, 'I thought you said you'd shot them,' to which he replied, 'I thought you said there was no one available?'

A man from Bathpool in Taunton rang in to Avon and Somerset Police to report that someone had just put excrement through his letterbox. He rang back some minutes later to cancel any police unit, as he had determined that the excrement was in fact peanut butter. 'Are you sure?' the operator asked him, to which he replied, 'Oh yes. I've tasted it. It's definitely peanut butter.'

A frantic female caller rang 999, stating to the operator, 'I can't find my death certificate.' The operator didn't know whether to send round a police officer or an undertaker.

One night a scruffy Cambridgeshire police dog handler attended a hostel for the homeless to assist staff in evicting a violent vagrant from the premises. On the dog handler's arrival, police were already on scene and speaking to staff. The dog handler then went into the hostel to carry out a search for the vagrant. As he was walking through the building he was tapped on the shoulder by a member of staff. 'Excuse me,' he said, 'I've not seen you before, which room are you in?'

A man rang Taunton Police Station to report the theft of his tax disc from his car. When asked his address, the man said, 'Go up the road, past the fish shop, turn up that road that goes past the place that sells a lot of things, then up the hill. You can't go wrong. It's Brian's Street.' Asked if he was sure it was Brian's Street, the man replied, 'Yes, Brian lives just down the road.'

A bemused police operator received a 999 call from an anxious female who asked if the weather would hold, as she wanted to wash her curtains.

A lady attended Taunton Police Station to report a lost dog. She had just collected it from the RSPCA dog pound, who had insisted that she place a six-foot fence around her back garden. At some cost, she had done as advised. She told the officer how she had shown the dog its new home, whereupon it had promptly jumped the brand-new six-foot fence and ran off. Asked for the name of the dog, she replied curtly, 'An ungrateful bitch.'

Late one night a woman phoned up a police control room asking, 'The seagulls are keeping me awake. Can my friend shoot them?'

A man handed a mobile phone into a police station, having found it by the roadside. When asked by the station PC how he found it, the man stated that he had seen it lying by the road, picked it up and answered it after it rang. On answering, a male voice had said, 'You've got my f*cking phone, you wanker! Take it to the f*cking police station now, you c***!' A good citizen, he had done as requested. As the man turned to leave the PC asked, 'The phone is smashed to bits. How the hell did it ring?' 'Someone must have driven over it, officer. It's a very busy road,' replied the male, smiling as he left.

A male caller phoned up Taunton Police Station, enquiring about a local campsite. He asked, 'Is it a 24-hour site?' to which the station officer responded, 'No, they throw everyone out at night.'

One morning, PC Ken Edge received a report that a gardener had been viciously savaged by a dog and required hospital treatment. PC Edge soon learned that this was not the first occasion that the animal had bitten someone. No incidents had previously been reported, but the outrage caused numerous other residents to come forward and make similar complaints and PC Edge was tasked with taking their complaints. Dave the postman was the last victim to come forward.

Dave explained to the PC that he had been delivering mail on the Dagenham estate when the wretched animal had confronted him. Fearing for his life, he had flung his sack onto the floor and run to the nearest house, where he

131

had battered frantically on the door. After some time and much gnashing of teeth, a bleary-eyed, unshaven householder had opened the door and the terrified postman had rushed past him into the house, where he spilled out his story. After a brief pause, and without a word, the householder, shoving his raincoat over his pyjamas, had gone to the end of the garden and retrieved Dave's mailbag. Ignoring the postman's dishevelled and bloody appearance with callous indifference, he had then handed Dave the bag, saying, 'Best be on your way now, people might be waiting for their post.'

At this point, PC Edge put down his pen. 'Didn't he offer any first aid?' 'No, nothing,' Dave said, gloomily. 'Cup of tea? Use of the phone to ring the sorting office or 999?' the PC asked, shocked. 'No, nothing. No help at all.' Shaking his head, the PC finished taking the statement. A few days later he was relating this very tale to the local Neighbourhood Watch Coordinator with particular emphasis on the unhelpful resident. The lady began smiling knowingly. 'You know him?' PC Edge asked. She nodded. 'Bill's not so bad really.' 'Didn't strike me that way,' said the PC. 'Bill's not been his old self since his wife ran off six months ago,' she replied. 'That's no reason to behave the way he did,' said the PC indignantly, to which she answered, 'Perhaps you'll take a less harsh view of him if I tell you that the bloke she ran off with was a postman.'

An elderly male called in to report a vehicle being driven erratically along a main road in Taunton in suspicious circumstances. He told the station sergeant that the young male driver had a female in the car who had her head buried in the driver's lap and that the driver had his hand on the woman's head. The elderly gent stated that he thought she was being held against her will. He was not impressed when the sergeant told him with smile that the matter would be looked into on a non-urgent basis.

A male law student phoned police to report the recent theft of his mountain bike: 'Police will be able to recognise it because I put my postcode on a piece of paper inside the tyres.'

A female caller phoned into her local police station and told the PC at the front desk that she was going to a wedding in Taunton but had lost her invitation. She couldn't contact the bride's mother and did not know any of the other guests. Could police let her know where there were weddings being held that weekend in Taunton?

A few years ago, PC Tony Broughton of Spennymoor Police Station was on night shift in the control room when he was asked to summon the police helicopter to assist officers on the ground that were chasing car thieves. The helicopter duly turned out and from his seat in the control room the PC could hear it flying around the town in a circular flight path assisting in the search. A short time later, a little old lady phoned in to ask PC Broughton if he knew there was a helicopter flying around the town. When the PC politely told her it was a police chopper searching for somebody, the old lady replied, 'Well, can't you get in touch with the pilot? I think he must have fallen asleep because he's just flying round and round.'

PC Harry Morris was walking the beat in the Cotswold village of Broadway when he came across a large number of tourists. He was approached by an American woman and her four-year-old son. She asked him whether he would be willing to pose for a photograph with her son and, in the interests of good public relations, PC Morris naturally agreed. As he took the child's hand, however, the boy looked distinctly apprehensive. The mother, noticing this, said, 'Now, don't worry son. This is not a real cop. This is an English bobby.'

Traffic PC Storey was on patrol with his colleague one night in Durham during the early seventies. Stopping at a set of lights at about 1 a.m. they saw a coal lorry shoot over the bridge, narrowly missing their stationary police car. Immediately behind the coal lorry was a pursuing police van, its blue lights flashing. PC Storey then joined the chase.

They followed the police van over the hill and found it parked behind the lorry, which had just crashed through a wall and was now hanging over the banks of the River Wear. The other officers were dragging the four young male occupants from the (stolen) lorry. PC Storey took two of the prisoners to the station, where he noticed that one of them, a smartly dressed lad in a suit, appeared to be quite ill. The youth was white as a sheet and shivering uncontrollably. PC Storey asked him if he was all right, at which the youth explained that he was a law student and had been walking back to college when the lorry had stopped and asked him the way to the motorway. He'd said he was going that way and was told to jump in. They had then come across a police van and the fun had started.

An elderly lady rang her local police station one evening and made the following complaint: 'There's a loud noise coming from the flat above ... I get it every night.'

Detectives in Clapham were carrying out extensive observations for the best part of a month on a lock-up garage situated next to a rather squalid public toilet with the usual reputation. While officers were keeping round-the-clock observations on the premises, they noticed that every morning without fail a smartly dressed man would walk into the toilets carrying a loaf of bread under his arm. Seconds later he would appear without the bread and walk on up past the concealed officers to the nearby train station, where he boarded a train. The man then returned at around 6 p.m. every evening and was seen by police to go into the public toilets and walk out carrying the same loaf. Although it had absolutely nothing to do with the job in hand, the puzzled detectives had no idea what was going on, so on the last day of the their job they decided to satisfy their curiosity at this seemingly bizarre behaviour.

Sure enough, that morning the man was seen to walk into the toilets with his loaf of bread and to emerge some seconds later without it. As the man walked off towards the train station, the detectives decided to go into the lavatories and investigate. They quickly located the loaf, which had been perched on top of a toilet tank in one of the many cubicles. With the penny beginning to drop, the officers awaited the return of the man and confronted him at 6 p.m. as he went into the toilets to retrieve his loaf. Asked just what the hell he was doing, the man sheepishly replied that bread was extremely good at absorbing aromas. The disgusted officers decided not to ask the man what he did with the bread when he finally got home.

Police were asked by ambulance control to attend an address in Nottingham Road following a report of a man cutting his private parts off. Soon afterwards, one of the attending PCs called up over the radio to say that the man was now at the hospital and that they were leaving it in the hands of the staff nurse ...

A concerned woman phoned her local police during the early hours to report that someone had just pushed a motorbike up her back passage.

Police received a letter from a member of the public reporting an incident. It read as follows:

Dear Sir/Madam

I apologise for not reporting this in person, but I am a bit embarrassed by what happened. Last Saturday I went out with my next-door neighbour to a local pub. I have known him for several months but I must admit we had only ever exchanged pleasantries. I accepted his offer of a night out as I am new to the area and to be honest was feeling a bit lonely. We spent the evening drinking and chatting and he invited me back to his house to watch a video. We got back to his house and he went into the kitchen to make me a cup of coffee, as I was feeling a bit drunk. Seconds later he returned without the coffee sat beside me and grabbed hold of my chest area. Shocked I jumped up and away from him. He stood up, dropped his trousers, revealing his erect penis. He then shouted, 'Come on, you know you want it. You're giving out all the signals.' Terrified, I ran out of the house and back home. I would be grateful if an officer could call round and see me to discuss what action I can take against my neighbour.

Yours faithfully,
Mr Bernard Knight

A young female phoned into Nottingham police control room to report, 'My boyfriend has thrown me out of the house and I'm completely naked, can someone help me?' It is believed the world and his wife turned up to assist her.

Police operators in Nottingham were told by an anxious lady, 'Me and my daughter have just seen a man put his private parts through our letter box ... we don't know who he is.' Meanwhile, on the same night, a man rang in reporting that his neighbours were going absolutely barmy and 'could a unit attend as the language they are using is f*cking terrible'.

CHAPTER FIVE

INTERVIEWS

In order to be a good liar, you need to have a good memory. Fortunately, this is not an attribute possessed by most run-of-the-mill villains. Sad to say, neither is it a quality possessed by some police officers. The knowledge that everything you say is being tape-recorded and may be played before a court is often enough to reduce the most confident of people to a nervous wreck.

Surrey PCs Brennan and Pearce were conducting a tape-recorded interview of an eccentric villain who was suspected of having committed a deception at a Weybridge restaurant. PCs

Brennan and Pearce introduced themselves and requested that the suspect state his full name and date of birth, which he did. PC Brennan then said, 'Can you confirm that there are no other persons present in this interview room?' The suspect replied, 'That's correct, except of course for the Almighty.' PC Brennan, slightly confused, replied, 'Who?' To which the suspect replied, 'God, of course. He's here. He's all around us.' PC Brennan then replied, 'Well, I won't ask him to state his name and date of birth.'

A scruffy shoplifter caught red-handed by PC Brennan stealing over £100 worth of L'Oreal shampoos and cosmetics from a large supermarket in Surrey was asked why he stole £100 of L'Oreal goods when he could have afforded the £30 for the supermarket's own brands. The shoplifter scratched his lice-ridden, matted, greasy hair and replied, 'L'Oreal, because I'm worth it.'

PC Clarke, a nervous young probationer constable, had cause to enter an interview room in which he believed there was a taped interview in progress. On entry he stated his name and announced, for the benefit of the tape, his reason for interrupting. Almost without breath he then declared for the benefit of the tape that he was now leaving the room. At that point the interviewing officer stated, dryly, 'For the benefit of PC Clarke, the tape is not running.'

A young DC tasked with dealing with a particularly nasty robbery was in the interview room when his detective sergeant returned from a rather lengthy luncheon. 'What's he got to say for himself, then?' the DS asked his subordinate, glancing with disdain at the man sitting opposite the DC. 'Well Sarge,' the DC answered, 'not much at the moment.' 'Is that so?' said the DS, and with that he went up to the male, grabbed him by the throat and brought his hand back into a fist. 'Let's see what he's got to say in a minute then, shall we?' 'Sarge,' the DC cut in, horrified, 'that's the victim!'

Whilst waiting to be interviewed at Guildford custody, a slow-witted prisoner with learning difficulties turned to his appropriate adult and complained, 'The police searched absolutely everywhere in the house, every crook and cranny.'

During the late seventies and early eighties, before interviews were tape-recorded, a lot of very strange practices emerged. In the West Midlands tales of a white rabbit emerging from cupboards in interview rooms began to circulate. Apparently, when a defendant refused to admit his guilt, this white man-sized rabbit would emerge from a cupboard and belt the prisoner around the head, say, 'Tell the truth', and then go back into the cupboard. The interviewing officers would act as if nothing had happened. When asked by the prisoner who the white rabbit was, the officers would say, 'What white rabbit?' It all finally came to light when one such prisoner told a packed Birmingham Crown Court that the only reason he had admitted the offence was because a white rabbit kept coming out of a cupboard and hitting him. To this day the white rabbit's identity remains a mystery.

Two local thugs were out in their battered Ford Fiesta early one evening when they came across a couple of smartly dressed young men on foot close to their rural home town of Anglesey in North Wales. The thugs, deciding to have some fun, stopped their vehicle and promptly set about the pair, hospitalising them both. The local police were duly informed and supplied with the vehicle registration number and very soon afterwards both thugs were in custody and interviewed. Both their stories followed the same line, that they had been out driving when two men had jumped in front of their car, forcing them to swerve; that when they had stopped and approached them, they were instantly attacked by the two highly agitated and drunken out-of-towners. Fearing a car-jacking, they had reciprocated by using minimum force before immediately leaving the scene. The interviewing PC Jennings then began to read from the victim's witness statements as follows: 'As part of our training to enter the priesthood, it is necessary to visit the local parishioners in designated areas' etc. etc. Suffice to say, the thugs changed their story and coughed the lot.

CHAPTER SIX

COURT

Giving evidence before a court is probably one of the most stressful tasks police officers are required to undertake and, as such, the potential for verbal gaffes is immense. Such mistakes are not just confined to the poor PC sweating in the witness box and many an over-educated barrister has underestimated his uniformed quarry, as the following tales illustrate.

A frequent visitor to a London magistrates court was on trial after being found in possession of a knife by a seasoned PC. Throughout the trial he denied having the knife and accused the officer of fitting him up. The man was found guilty by the magistrate and, due to his string of convictions for violence, including assault on police, he was sent to prison for three months, much to the delight of the arresting officer. The officer was then beckoned over to the magistrate, who leaned down and whispered in the PC's ear, 'Constable, I never want to see that knife in this courtroom again. This is its third appearance this year.'

PC Quentin was giving evidence in a major drugs supplying case at Knightsbridge Crown Court in London. He was in charge of all the exhibits, which consisted of scales, money, silver foil, used needles and other unsavoury articles. He told the judge that the Metropolitan Police forensic science laboratory had examined all these exhibits and in his words, the lab was 'The foremost forensic science lab in the world'. He went on to say that in the opinion of the lab, the exhibits were so contaminated with residues of heroin that any innocent member of the public coming into contact with them may absorb them through the skin and would suffer harmful effects. For this reason PC Quentin suggested that he be allowed to show the jury the various articles. The judge immediately agreed with PC Quentin and told him that he had best take the items around the jury box personally. PC Quentin then slowly put on a pair of rubber gloves and carefully showed each member of the jury the various exhibits, being cautious not to accidentally touch anyone with the items. The jury were fascinated and several asked to view the items from various angles. Upon returning to the witness box PC Quentin put each hand to his mouth and pulled off the rubber gloves with his teeth, much to the horror of the judge and jury.

A brand-new probationer on his first visit to crown court stood shaking with nerves in the witness box to give evidence and after giving the oath, he finished with, 'Your Majesty.' The judge replied, 'Not quite, officer, just "your Honour" will do.'

An ageing PC with only two days to retirement decided to put his language skills to the test during a trial at a Surrey magistrates court. A German tourist stood accused of being drunk and disorderly and the interpreter had failed to turn up. In an effort to get the very simple case out of the way before lunch the magistrate asked if there was anyone in the building that could speak German. Not wishing to miss such an opportunity, the PC kindly offered to assist. Walking up to the defendant, he said loudly, 'Vot ist your name?'

Some years ago in Oxted Magistrates Court, a case concerning the theft of coal from a local supplier's yard was being heard. The complainant was in the witness box giving evidence and was questioned by the defence solicitor as to the exact weight of coal allegedly stolen. The defence brief asked the complainant how he knew that he had had the coal stolen. The complaint explained that the coal had just been delivered and he had noticed a quantity missing from the pile. The defence then went on to suggest that it was impossible for the complainant to say the exact weight and quantity of the coal that he stated was taken. The complainant insisted that he could say the weight and quantity, as he had been in the industry for more than twenty years. At this point the prosecution solicitor turned to the court usher and said, 'Can you get me stones?'

150

The usher left the court, returning five minutes later carrying a selection of rocks in his arms. The surprised prosecution solicitor then said, 'What are you doing?' to which the usher replied, 'You asked for some stones.' 'I meant the Stones law manual,' sighed the solicitor.

WPC Pathan was on patrol with DC Batley when, approaching some traffic lights, they saw a male drive straight through a red light. The male was stopped and given a fixed-penalty ticket, which he disputed, and the case ended up at court. Giving evidence, WPC Pathan was asked whether she had actually seen the defendant go through a red light. She replied, 'No.' When asked why she had written in her notes that she had seen him go through a red light she replied, to the horror of her colleague, 'Because the DC told me to write it.'

A DC called Geoff was involved in a prolonged trial with a gang of burglars who were up for burglary and conspiracy. The trial, which was in its second week, was being held before the honoured Judge Black, DSO, DFC (a former World War Two bomber pilot). The defence was accusing the DC of systematically beating up and torturing one of the defendants over a period of four days. 'Officer,' began the barrister, 'I have noticed throughout this trial you have been wearing that particular tie, is there a reason for this?' Before the DC could answer, the barrister continued, 'Officer, isn't it a fact that it is a Karate Club tie, which would uphold the allegations of assault my client has made against you?' Before the DC could open his mouth, Judge Black immediately intervened. Moving his bifocals to the tip of his nose, he leaned over the bench, glared at the barrister, and thundered, 'That tie this officer is wearing, he is no doubt proud to wear, sir. It is not a Karate Club tie but in fact a Royal Air Force tie.' The barrister replied, 'Er, no further questions,' and sat down quickly.

All the defendants were found guilty. The DC, ex-RAF himself, from then on made sure that he always wore that tie before Judge Black.

A PC attended a domestic incident at which he found out that the ex-boyfriend of the distressed victim was phoning up and making threats to kill her and her family. Luckily, the father of the victim, who was an electronics buff, had managed to record the threats onto tape and the suspect was subsequently arrested. At court, the defendant pleaded not guilty to making threats to kill and the trial began. The defence solicitor called the victim to give evidence. She broke down in the witness box but gave her evidence, followed by the officer involved and several witnesses. The magistrates heard the tape recordings and finally the defendant's turn came to give evidence.

The defence solicitor began questioning his client with the opening statement, 'You are not denying making the telephone calls, as we have heard on the tapes, but when you spoke to the victim, did you really believe that she would take your threats seriously?' The defendant turned to the magistrates to answer, as instructed by his solicitor, and said, 'Yes I did. I wouldn't have said it if I didn't mean it.' The defence solicitor glared at his client and attempted to rephrase the question and get the defendant to change his answer, but the defendant again repeated his answer to the magistrates.

At this point the trial was stopped by the head magistrate, who proclaimed to the defence solicitor, 'I do believe your client has just pleaded guilty.' The defendant was promptly given the maximum sentence possible and led down to the cells, where he suffered a verbal assault by his own solicitor who was overheard to say, 'I've defended some right dickheads in my time, but you're the biggest dickhead I've dealt with by far.'

PC Gamson, a nervous young probationer, was facing his first experience in the witness box at Staines Magistrates Court. Putting on a brave face, he followed the usher to the stand, where he was handed the Bible in his right hand and told to recite the oath. Things were going well until he pulled his notebook out from his pocket and a pack of flavoured condoms shot out and landed in front of the three elderly magistrates, one of who remarked, 'Church of England, then?'

A seasoned traffic PC was in court giving evidence against a motorist who was contesting a charge of excessive speeding. The defence solicitor was doing his best to discredit the officer in the box. 'Officer, just how fast was my client travelling when you decided to stop him?' asked the lawyer.

The traffic officer replied, 'Around 100 miles an hour, your Worships.' The defence solicitor then continued, 'And how do you know that my client was travelling at 100 miles an hour?' The traffic officer replied, 'I have ten years' experience as a PC, six of which have been as a traffic officer and I have driven numerous vehicles at high speeds. I know when somebody is breaking the speed limit.' The defence solicitor then hurled his pen across the courtroom and asked, 'Officer, in your expert opinion how fast was that travelling?' The traffic officer hesitated for a second before turning to face the magistrates and saying, 'I don't know, your Worships, I've never driven a pen.'

One morning a PC was giving evidence at magistrates court in a case involving a defendant who had been arrested and charged with abusive language likely to cause harassment, alarm or distress, the allegation being that the defendant had quite simply told the officer to 'f*ck off'. The defence solicitor argued that his client was merely speaking in his normal everyday manner in asking the officer to leave him alone. Much to the disbelief

155

of the constable, the magistrate in his summing up remarked, 'Officer, I am of the opinion that the defendant was conversing in his normal everyday working language and that he meant no offence. His colourful language is now in common use and no longer considered unacceptable to most people. I therefore find the defendant in this case not guilty.'

Strangely enough, the same PC was giving evidence later that day for a speeding charge in front of the very same magistrate who had acquitted his defendant that morning. When asked in the witness box how fast the defendant was going, the PC paused and, looking directly at the magistrate, replied: 'F*cking fast, your worship.'

During a trial at crown court for an armed robbery the investigating officer, a seasoned detective a week away from retirement, was giving evidence in the box and being cross-examined by a belligerent young defence barrister. 'Officer, did you call my client a c***?' Without hesitation, the detective replied, 'Yes I did, your honour.' There were gasps of astonishment from the jury. The surprised barrister continued, 'Officer, you admit to calling my

156

client a c***?' The detective replied, 'Yes, I did.' Sensing victory the barrister, who could hardly believe his luck, continued, 'Please explain to the court why you saw fit to call my client a c***.' The detective then turned to the jury and said, 'Certainly. Your client burgled a house and stole an antique shotgun worth over £14,000. He then cut off the barrel, making it worthless, and used this same gun to threaten innocent members of the public during a robbery. This robbery netted him a mere £500. Yes, your honour, in my opinion this man most certainly is a c***.'

A crown court judge was just about to sentence a man for a fraud offence. The defence barrister stood up and said, 'M'lud. I accept that my client has been found guilty of what, on the surface, is a serious crime. But I put it to you that no one has really suffered as a result of his actions apart from the insurance companies, who will no doubt cover their losses by adding a penny or two to their premiums for the next year. If you are considering a prison sentence for my client – and I say "if" because you may feel that probation is a suitable sentence – if you are considering a prison sentence, might I suggest that you be considering

a sentence in terms of months, rather than years.'
The judge looked at the defence barrister over his
glasses and said, 'Thank you, Mr Millington-
Smythe, I have heard what you have said and will
do as you suggest. I sentence your client to 72
months' imprisonment.'

A 69-year-old career burglar in poor
health had just been found guilty at court
for the umpteenth time in his life. The
judge sentenced him to four years in
prison. There was a loud gasp in the court
and the defence barrister shot to his feet
and said, 'My Lord, my client is 69 years old,
he will not survive a prison sentence of
that length.' The judge replied, 'Just ask
him to do as much as he can.'

A crown court case was brought to an
embarrassing adjournment halfway through a
trial because the absent-minded judge had
forgotten to bring his notes with him. 'I really
must apologise for this state of affairs, but
unless any of you have any suggestions we will
have to adjourn.' He looked at the barristers
and one of them said, 'Fax it up, m'lud.' To
which the judge replied, 'Yes it does rather,
doesn't it?'

In Stourbridge Magistrates Court, a dog handler was giving evidence in a disorder case. When he came to the direct speech of the defendant, he paused, realising there were ladies on the bench and said, 'I'm rather reticent to use the language of the defendant in front of ladies, as the defendant's language was rather foul.' The lady chair told the officer not to worry about them, they'd heard it all before, so he proceeded to give long evidence, effing this and effing that. This went on and on. The officer was obviously getting into the swing of it because towards the end of his evidence the prosecutor said to him, 'What happened then, officer?' and he replied, 'He kicked my f*cking dog, your Worships.'

A flustered police officer giving evidence in magistrates court was asked by the prosecutor, 'And what did the defendant say then, officer?' The officer looked towards the bench and said, 'He called me a worship, you c***s.'

Many years ago at magistrates court the chairman of the bench, having found a defendant guilty of affray, told him, 'We are going to send you to prison for three months, and if we had really believed the police officer's evidence, we would have sent you down for double that.'

Some years ago an inspector was prosecuting two men in magistrates court for being drunk and disorderly. He painted the scene: a busy marketplace where individuals were going about their lawful business in an orderly, well-fashioned, respectable manner; mothers were with their babies, grand-parents were with their grandchildren, all was serene. Then, turning and pointing at the two defendants, he said, 'It would have remained so, your Worships, but for the conduct of these two f*ckers here.'

One night, patrolling Jersey PCs Alan Aubert and his colleague were pursuing a car, which was swerving all over the road. The driver refused to stop and the PCs eventually followed the vehicle into the owner's driveway, where he was arrested for drink driving. The defendant pleaded not guilty and PC Aubert and his crewmate were called to give evidence at Jersey Magistrates Court. PC Aubert gave his evidence first and the defending advocate asked the usual questions. Did his breath smell of intoxicants? Was he unsteady on his feet? Etc. Happy with PC Aubert's answers, his colleague was then called to give evidence. After he had given his account the advocate asked the officer, 'What was my client's gait like?' to which the PC replied, 'We drove into the driveway so fast I couldn't see if your client had a gate or what at the entrance to his house.' The court had to be adjourned for the laughter to subside. The man was later convicted.

A detective sergeant was in court in the witness box and was asked if he had properly cautioned the accused. The DS appeared a bit flustered and the solicitor for the accused pressed him by asking if he could recall the exact words he had used at the time of the arrest. The DS was unable to do so and the case collapsed. Afterwards the detective inspector wanted to know what had happened. Had the detective sergeant forgotten the words of the caution? The DS answered, 'Oh no, sir. There are two cautions, the long one and the short one. The short one is "You're nicked." The long one is "You're f*cking nicked." The problem was, I'd used the long one.'

During a rape trial the victim, a timid sixteen-year-old girl, was being cross-examined in the witness box by the defence barrister. In an effort to prove that the girl was sexually active, the barrister held up a packet of condoms and said, 'Do you know what these are?' 'Oh yes, sir,' replied the girl. 'Then you have seen lots of these?' the barrister asked, smiling at the jury. 'Lots of them, sir,' said the victim, confidently. The barrister continued, 'And have you seen men using them?' 'Oh no, sir, never,' replied the girl, shocked. The barrister then said, 'What do you mean? You say you are very familiar with these but that you have never seen men using them. How can that be?' to which the girl replied, turning to the jury, 'Well sir, you see, I work in a chemists.'

Following a police raid on a brothel, an arrogant barrister was giving the arresting officer a particularly hard time in the witness box. The PC had told the court that he had burst into one of the rooms and found a couple lying on the bed. The barrister said, 'And they were having intercourse?' The PC replied, 'No sir, I said that I found them lying on the bed.' The barrister then shouted, 'Good heavens officer, you're a man of the world. What on earth do you think they were doing, riding a bicycle?' With a straight face, the PC replied, 'No sir, there was definitely no bicycle in the room.'

In the early 1950s, PC Ewens and his detective sergeant were giving evidence at Bridgewater Magistrates Court in a case involving two well-known villains, Smith and Shepherd. Both had a long string of previous burglary and theft convictions and had been charged with 'being in the possession of housebreaking implements by night', as the offence was known then. PC Ewens had given his evidence and was listening to the defending barrister cross-examine the DS. The barrister was being very careful to try to present his clients as good, upright citizens, without actually claiming that in so many words. (He knew that if he did not make such a claim their extensive previous convictions could not be made known prior to a guilty verdict being announced.)

The barrister was being very scathing regarding the implements that had been seized from the two defendants and

produced in court, namely a large screw-
driver, a bent nail file, a torch and a pair
of gloves. He held up each in turn and asked
the DS if he would be surprised to learn
that he himself often carried these items at
night, especially if called upon to repair
the chair of a friend, as Smith and
Shepherd had been. The barrister then held
up the items and said to the DS, 'I suppose,
Sergeant, you would arrest anyone you
found at night carrying these items?' The
DS replied in a slow, clear voice, 'No sir, I
wouldn't, but I would arrest the likes of
Smith and Shepherd.' The magistrates got
the point and the two were found guilty.

CHAPTER SEVEN

DEATH

No police officer enjoys dealing with death. Unfortunately, it is an aspect of the job that cannot be avoided. The only way to cope with this is to use humour as a shield. This is why the police have developed an infamous strain of what can only be described as black humour. Particular note is to be paid to the mortuary tale at the end of this chapter. At the time of writing, over twenty officers from police forces across the UK have claimed to either be the victim or the perpetrator in this story. We strongly suspect it to be a police urban myth and advise all police officers that value originality never to utter this tale again.

PC Brennan and PC 'Chalky' White were dealing with a particularly smelly dead body. In fact, so smelly that PC Brennan refused to go inside the house for fear of parting with his recently eaten dinner. The person had died while sitting in his kitchen on a chair, blocking the kitchen door slightly. Chalky offered to help the undertakers move the 20-stone corpse, which had been festering for a fortnight in the centrally heated house. As they attempted to move the body, the right foot – which was stuck to the floor – fell off, causing a gush of blood and fluids. Chalky and the undertakers ran outside to escape the stench. At this point the on-call doctor arrived, to officially certify death. PCs and undertakers advised her that the stench was horrendous and the male clearly dead, but the doctor ignored this and insisted in going inside the kitchen to carry out her various checks.

She pushed her way into the kitchen through the obstructed doorway, catching her handbag strap in the door as she did so. 'Oh my God,' she screamed as she tried to get out of the kitchen, her handbag strap stopping her. Tearing the strap free she ran out, retching and coughing. PC Brennan then laughed. 'What's the verdict, Doc? Is he dead?'

Metropolitan PC John Corkett was running a course for newly recruited probationer constables. PC Corkett discussed various methods that people use to commit suicide, namely hanging, drowning, overdose, razor blades etc. Another instructor then mentioned that the last suicide he had dealt with involved a man who had killed himself by putting a hosepipe through the window of his car. Most of the probationers nodded in clear recognition of this method of death, apart from one. He sat there with a very puzzled look on his face. Eventually he put his hand up and asked, 'Didn't the car leak? I mean, it's very difficult to drown yourself in a car.'

A young PC was given the grim task of delivering a death message to a distraught female. He sat her down and said, 'Your husband was involved in a car accident earlier today. I am sorry to have to tell you, but he's dead.' The female replied tearfully, 'He's been run over before, but never that bad.'

A cynical detective inspector was summoned to attend a press briefing following the gruesome discovery of a body, which had been cut up into nine pieces and dumped in a skip. A junior member of the local press asked, 'Inspector, are you treating this death as suspicious?' He replied, 'Yes. If not, it's the worst case of suicide I have ever seen.'

Some years ago, police were called to a suspicious death: a drunken man had run out of a local pub and jumped over the car park wall. Sadly, the male was not aware of the huge drop on the other side of the wall. Ever since, the pub became known to police as the 'Drop Inn'.

An old lady had died upstairs in bed and PC Bardell was sent to her country cottage to deal with matters. On arrival, he noticed the cottage consisted of two rooms connected by a very small winding staircase. The rooms were less than six feet in height and the PC had difficulty standing upright in them. Reflecting that he'd visited submarines with larger stairs, he quickly realised that getting the dead body down from the bedroom was going to be a problem. Added to this was the old lady's daughter, who was sitting in the living room, totally distraught after learning of her mother's death. Speaking with the elderly undertaker, who looked like he already had one foot in the grave himself, they decided to place the body in a canvas body bag rather than the usual box in order to get the body down the winding stairs. The last thing PC Bardell wanted was for the daughter to come upstairs and see them dumping her mother into a body bag. The identification of the deceased could wait until it was safely downstairs.

The body was placed in the bag and they carried it across the landing to the staircase. PC Bardell took most of the weight from the top end as they descended. The undertaker was having far more difficulty and, when nearly at the bottom, he slipped and let go of the bag. Feeling his back strain under the load PC Bardell let go of his end and the bag shot round the last bend of the stairs, crashing straight through the living room door, where it came to rest at the feet of the old lady's daughter. The bag stopped but its contents did not, and the old lady shot out of the end, head first. 'Mother!' screamed the daughter, promptly fainting. PC Bardell then turned to the undertaker and said, 'Well, that's sorted out the identification.'

A suspect for a burglary was being booked into custody by the custody sergeant. The conversation went as follows:

Custody officer: 'Have you ever, whilst in custody, attempted to harm yourself or attempted suicide?'

Suspect: 'Yes, I tried to kill myself, but I won't do it again.'

Custody officer: 'I shall have to take your belt and shoe laces from you to prevent you harming yourself.'

Suspect: 'You don't have to do hat because I won't try it again, honest.'

Custody officer: 'You have attempted suicide in the past, so I have to take these items from you for your own safety.'

Suspect: 'I promise you, I won't try it again.'

Custody officer: 'How do I know that you won't try it again?'

Suspect: 'Well, it frightened me so much last time that I won't try it again, I nearly died.'

A male reported a theft from his motor vehicle parked at the crematorium. Asked for his occupation, he told the controller, 'Heating engineer.'

Called to the scene of a possible suicide with his detective sergeant, the young new detective inspector of Folkestone Police Station found himself confronted by a rather stale corpse. Realising that they would need to take some rudimentary precautions, they retreated outside where the DS produced a cigar from his pocket. He then proceeded to break a small piece from the end of the cigar. 'Seen this in the films, Guv,' he explained as he placed a piece first in one nostril, then in the other. He then produced a packet of a well-known brand of small mints from the other pocket. 'Mint, Guv?' he asked, offering his colleague the packet. 'Oh, right, thanks,' said the DI. 'Two's fine,' he said, and then began to place one in each nostril. 'You're meant to eat the mints, Guv,' said the DS.

Kent PC Peter Booker was sent to a suspicious death in the hot summer of 1976. The deceased had been found in a tin hut near a disused chalk pit in Wouldham. The smell had been rancid and the air thick with flies. His sergeant eventually relieved PC Booker, who then returned to the station, where he began chatting to the telephonist, who happened to be deaf. He told her he needed a strong drink after the last job. The telephonist nodded and handed him a half-empty bottle of brandy. She explained that the sergeant had just been in and left it on the desk, where she had accidentally knocked some over, as there was no stopper. The grateful PC took a large swig and immediately felt much better.

'Thanks for the drink, Sarge,' said the PC on his sergeant's return, pointing to the brandy on the desk. The sergeant then asked the PC if he had seen the large bluebottle floating in the bottle. He went on to explain that the bottle had been found at the scene of the suspicious death and that he had seized it for analysis in case the deceased had used it to commit suicide with some drugs that were also found. It seemed that the fly had fallen out of the brandy when the bottle had been knocked over. The PC's feeling of well-being quickly took a nosedive as he was taken off to hospital for the customary stomach pump.

Whilst serving at Chatham Police Station, PC Booker had to deal with Bill, a man who was forever phoning police and telling them he intended to commit suicide. Bill had made several botched suicide attempts from the roof of a shopping centre opposite the police station, but would never actually jump.

One day, PC Booker was with a colleague when they came across Bill on a green behind the station. He had a broken bottle with him and was making half-hearted attempts to cut his arm, but was making no impression. PC Booker's colleague then said to Bill, 'No, you do it like this', and indicated the insides of his wrists. Bill looked, said, 'Like this?', and immediately slashed both his wrists, which began bleeding profusely. He then threatened the PCs with the broken bottle, slashing out at them so they could not get near enough to disarm him, or give attention to his self-inflicted wounds. PC Booker turned to his colleague and said, 'You've done it this time, over to you', to which his colleague replied, 'Watch this', and gave Bill an almighty kick in the groin. At this Bill screamed, dropped the bottle and gave himself up. Bill survived, but the fright was enough to ensure that he never made any more attempts to take his own life, nor indeed to trouble the police with his nonsense.

PC Graham Lightfoot was working alongside WPC Smith when they were called to deal with a sudden death at Epsom District Hospital. Attending the Accident and Emergency department, the two Surrey PCs were taken to the resuscitation room, where a grim-faced nurse stood beside the dead body, which was lying on a trolley with its lifeless eyes staring and lips blue. Catching sight of the body, the female constable asked, 'Is he all right?'

A probationer, PC Boon, who joined the city centre police in Birmingham, was given a particularly torrid time by his shift and after ten weeks was a bag of nerves. Eventually he was approached by one of the old sweats on the shift and told that a brand new PC was coming to the rota and that he was to be the new target. PC Boon was delighted to hear this and readily agreed to be part of the first onslaught against the new probationer. A set of keys to the mortuary were conveniently held at the police station so that any bodies found overnight could be taken straight there. The plan was for

PC Boon to be taken to the mortuary and laid on a shelf in the fridge. The new probationer would then be shown to the mortuary and when the fridge was opened PC Boon would sit upright and scare the new boy witless.

PC Boon thought this a great idea and come the fateful night he was taken down to the mortuary and laid under a sheet. Lying in the dark he desperately tried not to giggle and give the game away. He wasn't happy about lying in the fridge with the corpses, but he knew it wouldn't be for long. Suddenly a very low voice emanated from the corpse lying next to him: 'Cold in here, innit.' PC Boon nearly woke the dead with his screaming.

CHAPTER EIGHT

A-Z OF POLICE JARGON

Cops 'n' Robbers wouldn't be complete without a section on British police jargon. All police officers will be familiar with most of the below terms and phrases used by officers of most ranks, not to mention villains, in their everyday working lives. Of course, some officers can take it a little too far and you might be forgiven for thinking that they have just walked off the set of The Sweeney. The list below should give those of you who are outside the job a final taste of what it's like to inhabit the strange, and occasionally frustrating, but still exciting world of the British police officer. Political correctness and good taste have dictated that a few of the more delicate examples of jargon be omitted in order for my still-serving co-writer and good friend to remain in the firm. Wouldn't want to upset the Pink and Fluffy or Nine o'clock Mafia now, would we?

ANTI – members of the public known to be anti-police.

AREA SEARCH, NO TRACE – police radio-speak meaning there are no trace of suspects at location so police unit resuming patrol, although can sometimes mean 'Can't be bothered to deal, next job please.'

APPOINTMENTS – police management speak for an officer's personal protective equipment (PPE) i.e. his baton, handcuffs, CS spray etc.

ASP – extendable telescopic iron baton which finally replaced the severely outdated wooden truncheon.

ATTITUDE TEST – an unofficial test allegedly applied by PCs to those who have committed minor offences usually involving road traffic misdemeanours. People who pass the attitude test usually escape censure with a warning or some friendly words of advice whilst those who fail are those who have been rude to police or who show no remorse for their transgression. These people are more likely to pick up fines or be summoned to court.

BAGMAN/CARRIER – someone's right-hand man.

BANG TO RIGHTS – where someone is caught red-handed and/or there is overwhelming evidence to convict them in court.

BEAK – magistrate.

BLUE LIGHT TAXI – when drunken off-duty officers are assisted by their on-duty colleagues in getting home safely.

BLUE ON BLUE – where an officer tries to stitch up a fellow officer.

BLUE ROVER – To 'Blue Rover' it is to misuse the police warrant card to gain free access to a nightclub. A foolish tactic, also known as 'briefing it', which has the potential to backfire.

BENT – a corrupt police officer.

BIN – custody, police cell, as in: 'to have one (a prisoner) in the bin'.

BIN IT – get rid of something.

BIRD – as in to do bird, to serve a prison sentence.

BLAG – armed robbery.

BLACK RATS – traffic cops, so-called as they eat their own, i.e. would book their colleagues for offences.

BLAT – to drive at speed.

BLUES AND TWOS – to drive a patrol car with lights and sirens activated, AKA 'to blue light it', a 'blue light run'.

BODY – either a corpse or more commonly (thankfully!) a person who has been placed under arrest.

BOSH – to finish a job or get a crime off your workload, to bosh it.

BOX IT OFF – to finish the job (as above).

BRASS, i.e.; top brass – officers of rank.

BRAVE Sir Robin – less-than-courageous PC, derives from the Monty Python film The Holy Grail.

BREAD-AND-BUTTER POLICING – simple, basic, training school-level policing.

BRIEF – a solicitor.

BRITISH BOBBY – affectionate, dated term for a police constable. People will often refer longingly to the halcyon days when British bobbies were supposedly on every street corner and crime was negligible. It's true that crime was low in those bygone days – however, people tend to forget that the good old British bobby was quite within his rights to give you a clout round the ear for your cheek. People also refer to Dixon of Dock Green. As we said before, if we remember rightly the main character was shot dead.

BROWN – heroin.

BROWN BREAD – dead.

BROWN NOSE – to suck up to management.

BUBBLE UP – to get in trouble, to inform on someone.

BY THE BOOK – to do something according to policy, a straight-laced officer.

CALL – an incident requiring police attendance.

CALL SIGN – the number under which a particular police unit, whether a constable on foot, or a patrol car, is identified over the police radio.

CAN – prison or custody cell.

CANTEEN CULTURE – management term to describe the banter, jokes and camaraderie once enjoyed by the rank and file PCs and which helped officers to deal with the rigours and stresses of the job. Still exists to an extent but driven more underground due to current political correctness.

CARROT CRUNCHERS – city police term for constabulary officers in the counties.

CARRYING – to be armed with a weapon of some kind.

CARRY THE CAN – to take the flack or blame for something.

CID – Criminal Investigation Department.

CIVVIE – a civilian who works for the police.

CIVVIES – plain clothes.

CHARLIE – cocaine.

CHIEF CON – the Chief Constable.
Chored – traveller slang for 'stolen'.

CHOKEY – prison.

CLARET – blood.

CLOCK, i.e. to clock – to catch sight of, can mean to hit.

COLLAR – to arrest.

COMMUNITY SERVICE – a non-custodial supposedly punitive sentence handed down by a court requiring the offender to complete some kind of task beneficial to the community. Remains popular with the criminals who may or may not turn up.

COPPER – police officer.

COUNTY BOUNTIES/COWBOYS – officers in the county constabularies, as referred to by their metropolitan colleagues.

COUGH – to confess to something, a confession.

COVER YOUR ARSE – the most important unofficial motto or mantra for modern-day UK policing.

CRACK DEN – a place used for dealing in crack cocaine.

CREW UP – to partner, to work together with a colleague on a shift.

CUFF HIM/HER – a directive meaning 'handcuff'.

CUSHY NUMBER – an office job or position away from the front line of operational policing.

CUSTODY – police cells where all arrested people are taken.

CV/ CAREER FODDER – a term used to describe the PCs out on the street who may sometimes be cruelly used by ambitious aspiring officers of rank as pawns and scapegoats in order to assist their own ascent through the rank system and to advance their careers.

DABS – fingerprints.

DESK POLISHERS – derogatory frontline term for those police and civilian staff who work comfortable office hours in a safe environment thus spends all their time on their backsides thus polishing office furniture.

DICK – detective.

DINOSAUR – officer approaching retirement.

DIPPER – pickpocket.

DO-GOODER – often used to refer to an interfering pedant with no understanding of real policing methods or the harsh realities of the war against crime; can be inside or outside the force.

DO HIS/HER LEGS – a phrase meaning to unfairly cause harm to an officer's career or reputation.

DOMESTIC – an incident often involving domestic violence usually between husband and wife

DOSS DOWN – hang out/sleep.

DOSSER – lazy officer. A dosser can also be a vagrant or tramp.

DOUBLE BUBBLE – Bank Holidays, usually meaning double pay.

DRUM – house, residence.

DYNAMIC DASHBOARD – an example of ludicrous management-speak for strategic deployment of police officers.

EMPIRE – police departments run by little Caesars, i.e. 'He has his own little empire.'

EYEBALL – to have eyeball on something or someone is to have them in your line of vision (or to have visual).

EX-JOB – someone who was once in the force.

FAG ASH LILS – lazy officers who spend more time smoking behind the station than policing.

FAST TIME – to do something which requires quick action and resolution.

FAST TRACK – an officer usually a graduate on accelerated promotion.

FATAL – a fatal incident usually resulting from a road traffic accident.

FEEL HIS/HER COLLAR – to arrest him/her.

FENCE – someone who handles stolen goods and sells them on.

FILL YOUR BOOTS – help yourself, get stuck in.

FILTH – the police.

FIRM – police force.

FIT UP/STITCH UP – to frame.

FLYING SQUAD – police armed robbery team, aka the Sweeney.

FORM, as in he's got form – a criminal record.

FRESH OUT OF THE BOX – new recruits/probationer constables.

FRONT LINE – to be in the front line is to be out policing the streets.

GAVER – a traveller/gypsy term for a police officer.

GEAR – drugs, stolen property.

GENERAL HINDSIGHT – someone who expresses an opinion on how things should have been done after the event, usually someone in rank. The term derives from the saying, 'General Hindsight never lost a battle, but to be fair, he was never there.' A derogatory term for those who flee the front line of policing before passing judgement from a position of safety on officers who are out fighting crime and their 'fast-time' decisions.

'GIVE ME A BROOM AND I'LL STICK IT UP MY ARSE AND SWEEP THE FLOOR FOR YOU AS WELL' – well-used complaint made by harassed operational PCs and sergeants.

GURKHA – an officer who takes no prisoners, i.e. never makes any arrests.

GOBBY PROBATIONER – a new recruit who thinks he/she knows it all.

GONE TO RAT SHIT – a job that's messed up.

GOOD COPPERING – good police work.

GOOD OLD BOY – an officer who knows the score and can be trusted by other PCs to do a good job.

GOOD SEEING TO – a kicking or beating.

GO PEAR-SHAPED – to go horribly wrong.

GRAFTER – worker, i.e. a productive police officer.

GRASS – an informer.

GRIEF – trouble.

GRIEFY JOB – a job that is likely to cause the officer in the case some trouble.

GTP area – a location whose populous supports the police, i.e. good to police.

GUV/GUVNER – boss, inspector or higher rank.

HALF BLUES – when an officer has removed his tie and shoulder numbers but who remains identifiable as a PC by virtue of his unfashionable shirt and strides.

HAIRY-ARSED – derogatory term for an unthinking PC.

HANDS ON – to be hands on with someone is to have to use a certain degree of force on that person.

HASH – cannabis.

HATCHET JOB – when an officer is unfairly dealt with or disciplined by management.

HEAVY – thug.

HER MAJESTY'S HOTEL – prison.

HIDING TO NOTHING – as in, to be on this is to be getting nowhere.

HOBBY BOBBY – a special constable who does the job for love.

ILLEGAL – abbreviation for illegal immigrant.

INNER SANCTUM – to reach this is to have gained at least the rank of sergeant. The phrase is believed possibly masonic in origin.

IVORY TOWER BRIGADE – those office-bound members of staff (both police and civilian) who may fire criticism at the frontline PCs from their places or safety or ivory towers.

JACK UP – to get a job or operation up and running, or to inject heroin.

JAILBIRD – prisoner.

JARGON – police slang, language.

JITTERS, i.e. to get the jitters – to feel fear.

JOB, i.e. he/she is Job, or to be in the job – to be in the police force.

JOBS A GOOD 'UN – a phrase meaning the task or case has gone or is going according to plan, has been resolved satisfactorily.

JOBSWORTH – pedantic, inflexible and ignorant officer who does everything according to the book and never bends the rules no matter what the situation or need.

JOINED-UP POLICING – typical management-speak for police working with other agencies to resolve a policing problem.

JUNGLE DRUMS – the grapevine.

JUNKIE – drug addict. Seen by many as selfish individuals that live off society and contribute nothing.

JURY NOBBLING – threatening or bribing jury members to deliver a certain verdict and influence a court case.

KEYSTONE COPS – usually amateurish and shambolic piece of policing.

KIT – any article of police equipment.

KNOCK AROUND – to beat up (used mostly in reference to domestic violence).

KNOCKED OFF – stolen.

KNOWN OR WELL KNOWN – persons with whom police are familiar and who usually have convictions.

LEAD – a promising line of enquiry.

LEAN ON – to apply pressure to a suspect.

LEAVE IT – command meaning desist.

LEGEND IN HIS/HER OWN MIND – any officer who wrongly believes themselves to be the best copper since sliced bread.

LICENSED PREMISES – Normally a pub, i.e. with license to sell alcoholic drinks.

LICKS, i.e. to give licks to – to beat up.

LODGED UP – an officer believed to be a member of a Masonic Lodge.

LOOSE CANNON – an officer who is either going to end up in trouble or who is labelled this by management if he attracts complaints.

LOSE THE PLOT – sadly, on occasion officers under increasing work pressures can suffer stress and overreact or lose their cool in certain extreme situations.

LOSER – the victim.

MAGIC WORDS – the words informing a suspect that he is under arrest for a particular offence, and the following police caution.

MANAGEMENT-SPEAK – particular ever-evolving phraseology used by officers of rank and those aspiring to promotion, often essentially meaningless, empty or unintelligible to the operational frontline PCs.

MANOR – particular ground or area covered by a certain police force or station.

MEAT WAGON – police van.

MICKEY MOUSE – fake.

MICKEY MOUSE JOB – a poor job.

MOODY – stolen.

MOODY JOB – an incident that is not going according to plan or has got out of hand.

MOP – member of the public.

MORNING PRAYERS – daily intelligence briefing officers attend at the start of their working day.

MOTOR – a vehicle.

MULTI-AGENCY APPROACH – management-speak for police working with other public bodies such as social workers to resolve a community problem or, more often than not, merely drinking tea and talking about it.

NARBIS – Cannabis.

NAIL – to successfully catch a criminal.

NICK – an arrest, to make arrest.

THE NICK – the police station.

NINE O'CLOCK MAFIA – non-operational officers, rank and civilians who work office hours and who may criticise the PCs out on the street.

NINE TO FIVE ASSASSINS – another derogatory term for the above.

NO-HOPER – a job with little chance of being solved, or one that is leading nowhere.

NONCE – a sex offender.

NO SMOKE WITHOUT FIRE – the belief, often unfairly held by some management, that the number of complaints an officer receives – even if malicious/unproven – suggest he/she is guilty of some wrongdoing.

NOT THE FULL SHILLING – daft, not quite with it.

NUTS WENT, as in 'His nuts went' – to lose one's nerve in a conflict. To, lose your bottle.

OBBO OR OBS – police observations on either a person or premises.

OD – drug overdose.

OFFICE WALLERS – yet another derogatory operational term for those much-loved office-bound police and civilian staff.

OFF WEP – an offensive weapon.

OFF THE RAILS – a police officer or member of the public who loses their mind or is out of control.

OIC – officer in the case. The officer in charge of or dealing with the matter.

OLD SCHOOL – officers who still operate and police to the old standards and who disregard the petty dictates of political correctness and recent legislation like the Human Rights Act.

OLD SWEATS – again, officers approaching retirement who know or believe they know everything about policing.

ON THE TAKE – a corrupt officer who accepts bribes or other illicit offers.

OP – a police operation.

OP – observation post.

OPEN PRISON – bizarre concept where prisoners are released into the community during the serving of a custodial sentence. Clearly a contradiction in terms.

OT – police overtime.

OTT – over the top.

PATROLS WILL BEAR IT IN MIND – when police tell people this about a problem they usually mean there is bugger all they can or will do about it.

PIG – derogatory term for a police officer. 'Bacon' is another highly original variation of this. Pigs are however, very clean, highly affectionate animals and the male of the species has an exceptionally long penis. 'Pig' is therefore a strange choice as an insult.

PINK AND FLUFFY – derogatory term used by PCs to describe liberal management policing styles and political correctness which requires that criminals should be treated with kid gloves and even as, believe it or not, our customers. Also used to describe those officers who adhere to these values.

PIPE AND SLIPPERS BRIGADE – officers who have their feet up and are no longer (or never were) interested in catching thieves.

PISS POOR – unacceptable.

PM – post mortem.

POLITICAL CORRECTNESS – liberal, chattering class prescriptive and oppressive political ideology currently dominating all public institutions and arguably every criminal's best friend.

POINT AND CLICK POLICING – basic and simple policing tasks.

POISON – an officer who makes false allegations against other officers.

POLAC – any road traffic accident involving a police vehicle.

POT HEAD – cannabis smoker.

PR – officer's police radio.

PREVIOUS – someone who has this has previous convictions to their name.

PRIORITY SHOUT – police radio-speak for an urgent assistance call.

PRO – as in 'They are pro-police', i.e. people who support the police.

PROBY – a probationer constable. PCs are probationers for the first two years of their service and during this period they can be made resign for no reason as they are not fully fledged constables.

PSD – Professional Standards Department: our fair-minded, impartial colleagues in the internal complaints department (formerly C&D, i.e. Complaints and Discipline).

PUFF – cannabis.

PUNISHMENT POSTING – when an officer is moved department or police station as a result of having supposedly done something wrong.

PUT THE SQUEEZE ON – to put pressure on.

QUICK CUFFS – new rigid American style handcuffs that have replaced the old chain ones.

RANK AND FILE – the PCs who are in the operational front line.

RED MIST, i.e. to see red mist – term used to describe an officer caught up by adrenaline and the excitement of events to the detriment of his decision-making.

REHAB ORDER – drug rehabilitation sentence imposed by the courts in preference to prison. Very popular with junkies who burgle to fund their addiction since there is minimal disruption to their 'working lives'.

RESULT – a satisfactory ending to a job or incident, usually involving an arrest and/or a successful court case.

ROLL AROUND – fight.

ROLL UP – police term to arrive at an incident.

ROTA – team, shift.

ROUGH UP – to use some force on someone.

RUBBER HEELS – Complaints and Discipline Officers, so-called as you are unable to hear them creeping up on you.

RUMBLE – fight.

RUNNER – someone who ferries drugs about on behalf of a dealer.

RUNNERS AND RIDERS – police jargon for who has crewed up with who and under what call sign on any shift.

RV – is to rendezvous with another police unit (vehicle or individual officer).

SAIL CLOSE TO THE WIND – to tread a fine line between legality and illegality.

SAFE HOUSE – a place of safety either for intimidated witnesses, or criminals.

SARGE – Sergeant.

SCAPEGOAT – someone who is made to take the flak for a mistake or cock up by management.

SCREW – prison officer.

SCREW – to steal from, burgle.

SCROTE – an unpleasant person, or criminal. Derives from the word 'scrotum'.

THE SCRUBS – Wormwood Scrubs Prison, West London.

SECOND BITE OF THE CHERRY – to have second go at something.

SECRET SQUIRREL – anything covert.

SECTION HOUSE – police accommodation used by poor probationers who can't afford to get their own home due to inflated house prices.

SEXY JOB – a crime investigation that detectives, rightly or wrongly, find particularly juicy and rewarding to investigate such as a robbery or murder.

SHAFTED – to be set up or unfairly disciplined.

SHARP END OF POLICING – the operational front line of policing, the streets.

SHITS – villains.

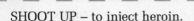

SHOOT UP – to inject heroin.

SIDE-HANDLED BATON – elongated metal
baton, which has replaced, along with the Asp,
the now obsolete wooden truncheon among
UK officers.

SKAG HEAD – Heroin addict.

SKIP OR SKIPPER – affectionate term for
one's sergeant.

SLAG – loser/criminal.

SLAMMER – police cell.

SLOW TIME – to carry out a non-urgent
enquiry when things are calm.

SMELLY JOB (or gone smelly) – a job featuring
hidden or developing complications with the
potential to get the officer disciplined.

SNEAKY BEAKY – an undercover officer.

SNOUT – an informant.

SOD THAT FOR A GAME OF SOLDIERS –
It's not worth it.

SOFT AS SHIT – physically or mentally weak.

SPIN THE DRUM – to search a
house/residence.

SPOTTER – an officer in plain clothes who is
dropped off at a location by a police unit to carry
out plain-clothes observations for that unit.

SPOUTS – lies, talks shit.

SQUAT – a building illegally occupied by
trespassers.

SQUEAL – to grass up someone, make an
admission to a crime.
STATION CAT – an officer who never leaves
the police station, also called Tiddles.

STICK ON – to discipline an officer or to report
someone for a traffic offence.

STIFF – corpse.

SUIT – detective.

SUPER – the Superintendent.

SUS – suspicious.

SQUARE UP – to quickly resolve a problem with no come back.

TAGGING – where an offender is electronically tagged as a means of monitoring him rather than him serving time in prison. Very popular amongst prison reformers, even more popular amongst the career criminals.

TEA LEAF – thief.

TELETUBBIES – plain-clothes undercover team.

THE TOP MAN – the Chief Constable or Commissioner.

THIEF TAKER – a good officer who catches criminals.

THIN BLUE LINE – the front line of operational PCs, which some would argue is on the point of becoming anorexic.

THOUGHT POLICE – to the paranoid, the politically correct Stalinist-like (well, almost!) elements within the police service who they believe seek to brainwash officers' minds and to attempt to control and legislate an individual officer's thoughts as well as his/her actions. Even the most innocent comment can fall foul of this sinister movement and invite swift discipline and punishment down on the unwitting transgressor.

TICKET, i.e. to get one's ticket – to be permitted to drive fast police vehicles.

TIT – PC's term for the world-famous police custodial helmet, which is loved and hated in equal measure.

TK – telephone box.

TOM – prostitute.

TOM DICK – to be off sick.

TOP AND TAIL IT – to finish a job or file properly.

TOP DRAW – a good job, thing.

TOOLED UP – to carry a weapon.

TOY TOWN POLICE – any county constabulary so-called by the metropolitan forces.

TREE HUGGER – an amusing derogatory term for the politically correct.

TROOPS – the foot soldiers, i.e. frontline officers. Bizarrely the word 'troops' is considered politically incorrect despite the fact there are many women serving in our armed forces today.

TUG – to stop/arrest.

UNIFORM CARRIER – an officer who has only joined the police to look good in the uniform and certainly not to catch villains.

UP THE ROAD – to go up the road is where a court case goes to crown court as opposed to the less weighty magistrates court.

WAYS AND MEANS ACT – fictional legislation by which officers jokingly justify slightly dodgy or questionable decisions.

WEENER – coward.

WET BEHIND THE EARS – probationers with no experience of operational duty.

'WHAT PART OF "NO" DON'T YOU UNDERSTAND?' – overused training school phrase.

WHEEL'S COME OFF – to go wrong.

WHIZZ – speed (illegal stimulant drug).

WOODEN TOP – Cockney rhyming slang for police officer.

WOOF YOUR COOKIES – to be sick.

WOOLLY LIBERAL – another word for a politically correct.

VERBALS – usually words uttered by arrested person after police caution.

VERBAL SOMEONE UP – to incriminate.

VICTORIAN COP – any officer with a pie and mash (moustache) who is particularly fond of

209

wearing the police custodial helmet, which has its origins in the Boer War and is therefore somewhat dated.

The authors are in the process of writing Cops 'n' Robbers 2 *and would like to hear from you if you know a funny tale which in any way involves the police. So, if you have a funny police tale which you would like to see in* Cops 'n' Robbers 2, *please e-mail it to* copsnrobbers@lycos.co.uk. *Anonymity and confidentiality are, of course, assured.*

The Victims of Crime Trust is a charitable organisation set up in 1994 by PC Norman Brennan to support victims of crime throughout the UK and to represent their interests. We would encourage any reader to visit their website for further information. It is worth remembering that there are a multitude of charities set up to represent the interests of criminals but a mere handful dedicated to assisting genuine victims of crime.

The Victims of Crime Trust
2 York Street
Twickenham
Middlesex
TW1 3LE

Reg. Charity No 1032867
Website: www.victimsofcrime.org.uk